Arthur Penrhyn Stanley

Sermons for Children, Including the Beatitudes and the Faithful Servant

Arthur Penrhyn Stanley

Sermons for Children, Including the Beatitudes and the Faithful Servant

ISBN/EAN: 9783744744980

Printed in Europe, USA, Canada, Australia, Japan

Cover: Foto ©Lupo / pixelio.de

More available books at **www.hansebooks.com**

SERMONS FOR CHILDREN

INCLUDING

THE BEATITUDES AND THE FAITHFUL SERVANT

PREACHED IN WESTMINSTER ABBEY

By ARTHUR PENRHYN STANLEY, D.D.

LATE DEAN OF WESTMINSTER

LONDON
JOHN MURRAY, ALBEMARLE STREET
1887

PREFACE.

These Sermons, having been found to interest many young persons into whose hands they came when privately printed, are now published in the hope that they may be of use to a wider circle of readers.

They have been reproduced as correctly as the rough state of the Author's Manuscript permitted: but it is obvious that, in some places, either the manuscript has been inaccurately deciphered, or the Preacher supplemented what he had written by additions at the moment.

The concluding Sermon, on 'The Faithful Servant,' though not addressed specially to children, and not preached in the Abbey, seemed from its personal and familiar character to have a proper place in this volume.

CONTENTS.

SERMON		PAGE
I.	THE CHILD JESUS (1871)	1
II.	LITTLE CHILDREN, LOVE ONE ANOTHER (1873)	10
III.	THE USE OF CHILDREN (1874)	20
IV.	THE 'GOLIATH' BOYS (1875)	32
V.	THE CHILDREN'S PSALMS (1876)	44
VI.	SICK CHILDREN (1877)	54
VII.	ST. CHRISTOPHER (1878)	67
VIII.	THE CHILDREN'S CREED (1879)	76
IX.	TALITHA CUMI (1880)	87
X.	THE BEATITUDES (1881)	95
XI.	THE BEATITUDES (1881)	104
XII.	THE BEATITUDES (1881)	113
XIII.	THE BEATITUDES (1881)	122
XIV.	THE FAITHFUL SERVANT (1856)	132

SERMONS FOR CHILDREN.

I.

THE CHILD JESUS.

(December 28, 1871.)

And the child grew, and waxed strong in spirit, filled with wisdom: and the grace of God was upon Him.—LUKE ii. 40.

THIS day is called the day of the Holy Innocents, because it calls upon us to remember the death of those little children who were killed at Bethlehem at the time of our Saviour's birth, when He also was a little child like them. It is also a day famous in this Abbey, because it was on this day, more than eight hundred years ago, that this great church was finished by its first founder, King Edward the Confessor, who was himself an innocent, guileless man, almost like a little child. We have thought, therefore, that it might be good to mark this day by gathering together here as many children as could come, and putting before them the example which our Saviour set to all children, He having been Himself a little child and a little boy, such as those who are here to-day. For this purpose the different passages of Scripture have been chosen that have been sung or read to-day; the eighth Psalm in order that you might see how little children may find out the glory of God in the great works of nature, the beautiful sights and sounds that they see and hear around them; the fifteenth Psalm in order to show how, from our earliest years down to our latest age, that in which God finds most pleasure is the humble, pure, truthful, honourable mind; and the one hundred and twenty-seventh Psalm in order to impress upon parents what precious, inestimable gifts are given to them in their little children. And the anthem has been chosen in order to remind all who are young how precious to them are the days of their youth, and how the one thing which they must bear in mind from first to last is to 'fear God and keep His commandments, for this is the whole duty of man;' and the hymn in order to show how all of us, even the youngest, may come to our gracious Saviour to ask Him to have pity upon us. And the lessons were chosen, the first in order to remind you how little Samuel knelt upon his knees at morning and evening, waiting for the voice of God to tell him what he was to do ; and the second lesson—which is what I will specially speak of now—because in it we have the example of our Saviour Himself as the little child. Let me, then, draw from these words what may be useful both for the parents and friends of those children who are here, and also, I hope, for the children themselves, if they will listen to what I say.

First of all it is said, 'The child'—that is, the child Jesus—'grew.' He grew in stature, and He grew in character and goodness. He did not stand still. Although it was God Himself who was revealed to us in the life of Jesus Christ, yet this did not prevent Him from being made like unto us in all things, sin only excepted. It has been reverently and truly said,—

> Was not our Lord a little child,
> Taught by degrees to pray ;
> By father dear and mother mild
> Instructed day by day ?[1]

Yes, He was ; we need not fear to say so, and in this lies the example for us. Each one of us, whether old or young, must remember that pro-

[1] Christian Year : *The Catechism.*

gress, improvement, going on, advance, change into something better and better, wiser and wiser, year by year—that this is the only condition, the only way of our becoming like Christ, and, therefore, like God. Do not think that you will always be, that you must always be, as you are now. No; you will grow up gradually to be something very different; you must increase and grow in mind as well as in body, in wisdom as well as in stature. The world moves, and you and all of us must move with it. God calls us, one and all, ever to something higher and higher, and that higher stage you and I and the whole world must reach by steadily advancing towards it.

And then come three things especially which the text puts before us as those in which our Lord's earthly education, the advance and improvement of His earthly character, added to His youthful and childlike powers. First, it speaks of His strength of character. It says, He 'waxed strong in spirit.' Strong! What a word is that for all of you, my dear children. You know—little boys especially know—how you value and honour those who are strong in body. The strong limb, the fleet foot, the sturdy arm, the active frame, you do well to value these things; they are God's gifts. The hardihood which can endure blows without flinching, and toil without fatigue, which can win the race, conquer in the game, or vanquish in the struggle of life—these are excellent gifts; and it is one of the worst evils of intemperance or dissipation that they spoil and destroy this glory of natural health and vigour which God gives to you. But it is not of this strength that the text speaks, or that I would now speak to you. What natural vigour is to the body, strength of character is to the mind. A stout heart, that is what you want—a stout heart which will be able to resist all the temptations to do evil, which scorns to tell a lie, which will never consent to be betrayed into doing what is wrong; a strong, hardy conscience, which fixes itself on matters of real importance, and will not trifle, will not waste its powers on things of no concern. Therefore, I say, be stronger and stronger every year. I could not say to you, perhaps, be stronger in body every year, for that is not within our own power, if we have it not; but I can say be stronger in spirit, be strong in mind, be strong in character, be stout in heart, for this does come by trying to have it. It comes by being always reminded that it will come if you strive to get it. It comes to those who are determined to seek it. Be strong, therefore, and very courageous.

And the next thing which the text speaks of is wisdom. It says the child was 'filled with wisdom.' Wisdom, as it were, was poured into Him, and His mind opened wider and wider to take it in. He drank in whatever wisdom there was in the knowledge of those about Him; He drank in the heavenly wisdom also which comes down from the fountain of all wisdom. You, too, have this to gain day by day. Those of you especially who are at school are sent to school for that very purpose, to have your minds opened, to take in all that your teachers can pour into them, to be ready for this instruction whenever it comes to you from books, from looking at what you see about you, from conversation, from experience as you grow older in life. You need not be old before your time, but you must even now be making the best use of your time. These are the golden days which never come back to you, which if once lost can never be entirely made up. Our great King Alfred used to regret in after years nothing so much as that, owing to his long wanderings and troubles when he was young, he had not had the opportunity of regular instruction at school. Seek, therefore, for wisdom, pray for it, determine to have it; and God, who gives to those who ask, will give it to you. Try to gain it as our Lord gained it when He was a child, by hearing and by asking questions. By hearing; that is, by being teachable, and humble, and modest, by fixing your attention on what you have to learn. And also by asking questions, as He did; that is, by trying to know the meaning of what you learn, by cross-questioning yourselves, by inquiring right and left to fill up the blanks in your minds. Nothing is more charming than to see a little child listening, not interrupting, but eager to hear what is taught. Nothing is more charming than to hear a little child asking questions. That is the only way in which we are able to know whether you take in what has been taught you.

And the next thing is the grace or favour of God, or, as it says at the end of the chapter, the grace, or favour, of God and man; the grace, the goodness, the graciousness of God, which calls forth grace, and goodness, and gratitude in man. Our blessed Lord had this always; but even in Him it increased more and more. It increased as He grew older, as He saw more and more of the work which was given Him to do; He felt more and more that God was his Father, and that men were His brothers, and that grace and loving-kindness was the best and the dearest gift from God to man, and from man to man, and from man to God. He was subject to his parents; He did what they told Him; and so He became dear to them. He was kind, and gentle, and courteous to those about Him, so that they always liked to see Him when he came in and out amongst them. So may it be with you. Look upon God as your dear Father in heaven, who loves you, and who wishes nothing but your happiness. Look upon your schoolfellows and companions as brothers, to whom you must show whatever kindness and forbearance you can. Just as this beautiful building in which we are assembled is made up of a number of small stones beautifully carved, every one of which helps to make up the grace and beauty of the whole, so is all the state of the world made up of the graces and goodnesses not only of full-grown men and full-grown women, but of little children who will be, at least if they live, full-grown men and full-grown women. Remember, then, all you who are parents; remember still more especially, all you who are children, remember this day; and if ever you are tempted to do wrong, or to be idle, or to be rude and careless, or to leave off saying your prayers, then think of your Saviour's good example which has been put before you to-night in Westminster Abbey.

II.

LITTLE CHILDREN, LOVE ONE ANOTHER.

(December 27, 1873.)

I write unto you, little children, because ye have known the Father.—1 JOHN ii. 13. *My little children, let us not love in word, neither in tongue; but in deed and in truth.*—iii. 18. *Little children, keep yourselves from idols.* v. 21. *I have no greater joy than to hear that my children walk in truth.*—3 John 4.

THE day on which this service is usually held is called Innocents' Day, from the little innocent children that were killed at Bethlehem. But as this year Innocents' Day falls on a Sunday, I have invited you here on this the day before, which is called St. John's Day, because it is the day on which we are called to think of the good apostle St. John. I shall say a few words to you about him. His memory was very deeply cherished by the good king who on Innocents' Day founded the Abbey, and it has been very dear to Christians always. When he was first a disciple of our Lord he was quite young, perhaps not much more than a boy. But there was something so winning about him that our Lord always kept him close to Him, and he was called the disciple whom Jesus loved. When our Lord was gone away into heaven, this disciple St. John, after living some time at Jerusalem with the other apostles, went to the great city of Ephesus, and there he lived on after all the other apostles were dead, and he was the only one left. There is a beautiful picture which some one has painted of the old man sitting on a rock quite alone, and looking up into heaven, and seeing there his former companions in that better world still busying themselves with doing good and holy things, as we hope that all those whom we have loved and admired on earth are doing still. It was whilst he was living there that various stories are told of him that we do not find in the Bible, and we cannot be sure that they are quite certainly true. But they are what the early Christians believed about him, and they agree so well with the letters or epistles which he wrote at that time, and from which I have taken the texts of this sermon, that I will try to tell them to you, and see what we can learn from them.

One is this. There came one day a huntsman who had heard so much of this great, wise old man, that he went out of his way to see him; and to his surprise he found St. John gently stroking a partridge which he held in his hand, and he could not help saying how surprised he was to see so great a man employed on anything so small. Then St. John said, 'What have you in your hand?' And he said, 'A bow.' And St. John said, 'Why is it not bent?' And the huntsman said, 'Because then it would lose its strength.' 'That is just the reason,' said St. John, 'why I play with the partridge. It is that my mind may be kept strong by sometimes being at play.' What do we learn from this story, my dear children? We learn from it that St. John, and great and good men like St. John, are glad now and then to see you at play, and to play like you. They are glad to see you happy; and they wish to be little children again like you, because that helps them afterwards to work better. We learn from it to be kind as he was to little birds and beasts: never to torment them; to remember that kindness to dumb animals is a part of what God requires of you. There was an aged lady, very excellent, wise, and wonderfully learned, who lived to be very nearly as old as St. John, and who died last year in her ninety-second year. She said, a very short time before her death, 'I hope that the time may come when children shall be taught that mercy to birds and beasts is part of religion.' Yes, it ought to be part of our religion. I trust that we shall make it so. Play, too, with your companions, like St. John; remember always that all play and all holidays are given by God, to be like the unbending of a bow, to help you to work better for the future. It is as when he said in his epistle, 'I write unto you, little children, because ye have known the Father.' You have known our loving Father in heaven. He gives you all good things, work and play, play and work, to make your minds and hearts stronger, and better able to do His will. He gives you beautiful birds and beautiful animals to play with and to love. They, too, are His creatures; He has made you their guardians and playmates, and he has made them your companions and teachers.

Another story is this. There was a young man who had grown up under St. John's care in doing what was right, and St. John was very fond of him. At last, after a time, St. John had to go away, and gave this young man in charge to the bishop or chief pastor of Ephesus, and told him on no account to let him go astray. But when St. John came back and went to the bishop, with whom he had left his young pupil, he saw from the bishop's face that something sad had happened. 'What is it?' he said; and the bishop told him how this young man had fallen in with bad companions, who tempted him away into the mountains, and there they were living the wild life of robbers, and used to come down from the hills, as the robbers still do, in those countries, to carry off travellers and ask a ransom for them. As soon as St. John heard this, he immediately set off into the mountains. He was not frightened by the thought of the robbers, he cared only to save this poor young man from his bad courses. And when the robbers saw him coming, they said amongst themselves, 'Here comes some one that we can carry off;' and down rushed the young man who had become their chief, and found himself face to face with his beloved old master and friend St. John. And the moment he saw him he burst into tears and fell at his feet, all his better feelings revived, and instead of his carrying off St. John, St. John brought him back to good ways, and he never went astray afterwards.

What do we learn from this? Is it not something like that which St. John himself said in that chapter which you have just heard? He had taught this young man as a little child to love and know the good Father of all. He had taught him as a young man to overcome the wicked one; that is, to get the better of the evil that there is even in the best things. And now when he went astray he never lost his interest in him; he went after him, even at the risk of his own life, to bring him back, and he succeeded. This story is full of instruction even for us. It brings back to us some of St. John's own words, 'Little children, keep yourselves from idols.' Although we have now no idols like those which the heathens worship, yet there are many idols still. If a little brother or sister will insist on having a toy for himself, and not let any one else play with it, that is his 'idol.' If any boy who is growing up thinks of nothing but games and amusement, and neglects his lessons, then games become his idol. If a young man goes, as did that one in the story, after bad companions, they become his 'idols.' Keep yourselves from all these idols; and all of you, O children, boys, and young men, remember that there is no greater pleasure you can give to your parents and teachers than to continue in the good thoughts and words that they have taught you; remember that there is no greater pain for them than to think that you have forgotten what they told you, that you have ceased to care for them, and have gone off into evil ways. And oh, how happy for you, how happy for them, if when you have gone astray, or done anything wrong, you come again like that young man and acknowledge your faults! and the good old friend, whoever it is, father, or uncle, or brother, or teacher, will receive you back again as if nothing had happened. 'I have no greater joy,' St. John said, 'than to hear that my children walk in truth.' Be truthful in all things, acknowledge your faults as did the young robber chief, do not keep them back from your parents or friends. Never tell a lie to conceal what you have done wrong. Have no tricks or schemes to make others think you better than you are. Tell the truth, and shame the devil.

There is one other story. When St. John was very old indeed, when he was almost a hundred, when he could no longer walk or speak as he had done in his youth, he used to be carried into the market-place in the arms of his friends, and the people, old, and young, and children, gathered round him to hear the farewell words of their venerable teacher. And then he would say, 'Little children, love one another;' and when they asked for something else, he said again, 'Little children, love one another;' and when they asked him yet again, still he said, 'Little children, love one another.' And they said, 'Why do you always say this, and nothing else?' And he said, 'Because this is the best thing I can say; if you love one another, that is all that I have to tell you.' What do we learn from this? We learn that the thing which St. John, the beloved disciple, was most anxious to teach, was that those whom he cared for should love one another. It is the same as when he said in his letter to them, 'My little children, let us love one another in deed and in truth.' And that is what we say to you now, 'Little children, love one another.' Little brothers, be kind to your little brothers and sisters. Boys at school, be kind to those who are younger and weaker than you. You can show them kindness and love in many, many ways; you can keep from teasing or hurting them, you can prevent others from teasing or hurting them; and that will make them love and be kind to you. Little boys will never forget the kindness they have received from bigger boys at school. Brothers and sisters who have given up lovingly and kindly when they were quite small will give up lovingly and kindly all their lives. Love one another in deed and in truth ; do not pick out each other's faults ; make the best of what there is good in each other ; be glad when you hear anything good of those who live with you. Never quarrel ; it does no good to any one. Never be jealous ; jealousy is one of the most mischievous, hateful things that can get into any one's mind. Never tell bad stories one of another. Never listen to bad stories of other people. When you ask to be forgiven in your prayers every night, always try in your hearts to forgive and forget what has been done to vex you in the day.

This is the love which St. John wished to see. This is the love which Jesus Christ wishes to see in all His disciples, old and young.

Always bear in mind that the first thing to be done is to try to help and befriend some one else. That will make you generous and just ; that will make you active and courageous ; that will make you feel how wicked it is to lead others into wrong, and how happy and excellent a thing it is to help others to be good. That will make you better able to love and to do good to men when you grow up to be men yourselves. That will the better enable you to love God, who can only be loved by those who love their fellow-creatures. Therefore I end this address to you, as St. John ended his long life, saying, 'Little children, love one another.'

III.

THE USE OF CHILDREN.

(December 28, 1874.)

And Jesus called a little child unto Him, and set him in the midst of them, and said, Verily I say unto you, Except ye be converted, and become as little children, ye shall not enter into the kingdom of heaven.—MATT. xviii. 2, 3.

THE Festival of the Innocents, which is the festival of little children, brings us in the course of the services of the Church to this incident in the Gospel history. Jesus called a little child, and set him in the midst of them. That is what is attempted here every Innocents' Day. We wish once a year to call the little children of London together and place them in the midst of this great church in this great metropolis, and ask them, and ask their friends and parents, what it is that these little faces ought to teach us, as they taught the first disciples of Jesus Christ.

First, what do they teach us about God and our Saviour? There was a very wise man, William

Paley, who lived a hundred years ago, who used to say that of all the proofs that the world gave him of the benevolence, the good-will of God, our Creator, the chief was the pleasures of little children. And there is a great deal in this: when we see the innocent, radiant happiness of children, without care and without sorrow, we cannot help thinking that we then see something like what is meant by Paradise, something like what God intended mankind to be. They are like the flowers, like the gay plumage and the flight of birds, like the dancing of brooks and rivulets; we cannot imagine why they should be as they are, except because God delights in such happiness, and would wish us to enjoy it. And so, too, in the Gospel history, where we hear how often our Saviour took notice of little children, how He set them up in the midst of His disciples, how He took them up in His arms and laid His hands on their little heads and blessed them, and by His outward gesture and deed declared His good-will towards them—this shows us how He enjoyed what we enjoy. It is the answer to the question which is sometimes asked—we hear that our Saviour wept, and we ask, But did He ever smile? Yes, He did smile. He must have smiled as He fondled these little ones. No one can mix thus with children, and not have his brow relax, and his eyes brighten, and his lips move with gaiety and laughter, as he handles them, and looks at them, and learns from them. And then, in this enjoyment and appreciation of little children, our Saviour teaches us the enjoyment and appreciation of all innocent happiness. He bids us enjoy this season. He bids us be as a child with children. He bids us be as little children. He bids us feel that He loves us as a father pitieth his own children. Surely the sight of little children set in the midst of full-grown men is a rebuke to our passions, a solace to our sorrows, an example for our imitation. 'Except ye become as little children, ye cannot enter into the kingdom of heaven.' No doubt there are bad children, there are vain children, who are no comfort and no examples to anybody ; but a good child is in some respects more of a comfort, more of an example, than a good man. And why? Because a little child knows nothing of our quarrels, of our doubts, of our disputes, of our ambitions, of our cares. It can come into a sick chamber, or a chamber of sorrow, when no one else can come in, because it awakes no painful feeling ; it is unconscious in its joy, it is gentle in its grief. It produces a holy calm which enables the sufferer to reflect and decide, and look upwards and inwards with the trustful confidence which the confidence of the child itself inspires. And do we not feel that in their presence, if anywhere, we are among those who see things as they really are?

And how often has a little child of a rough, hard father or mother, set in the midst of an unhappy household, been by its innocent ways the saving of such a parent or such a household! What protection there is in the smile of an innocent infant! What a sermon there is in the eyes of an inquiring, honest, fearless little boy; of a gentle, pure little girl! How impressive and how true to nature is the story of the old miser, Silas Marner, whose suspicious, irritable mind was gradually transformed and transfigured by the treasure of a little child that he one day found unexpectedly placed in his miserable home! That exactly expresses what our Saviour meant by setting a child in the midst of them. How striking the letter of Luther to his little boy John, or his letter on the death of his little daughter Magdalen! These children seem to have been given to him that all the world might know what a kind, tender heart there was in that strong, strict, energetic man. Or in the history of England is there any crime in the bloody civil wars of York and Lancaster, or any of the cruelties of the kings and barons in those savage times, which has so touched the hearts of all Englishmen in later days as the murder of the two little princes in the Tower?

> Thus lay the gentle babes girdling one another
> Within their alabaster innocent arms;
> . . . . . .
> A book of prayers upon their pillow lay.

We feel, as we read that story, a glow of righteous indignation against grasping ambition and selfish tyranny of every kind, past or present. Or in the history of the horrors of the French Revolution is there any deed of blood which has left so dark and deep a stain on the violent party-spirit and revolutionary fanaticism of those days as the inhuman treatment of that unfortunate child, the son of Louis XVI., who died at ten years old of the misery and insults inflicted upon him by the agents of the ruffians who then trampled on the liberties of France? I have seen an ivory cross, said to have been worn by the queen his mother on her way to the scaffold. But the figure on the crucifix is not the dying Redeemer in his full-grown stature, but the infant Jesus stretched on the cross, with His gentle smile and innocent gestures.

Whether or not it was that she, in that last hour, was thinking of her own unhappy child, that little figure at least represents what has been the feeling of humanity in the whole course of history—that there is nothing which so touches the heart, or elevates the thought, or stirs the just anger of the better portion of mankind, as the wrongs or the sufferings of a little child. Such thoughts as these ought to strike home to the hearts of all who have anything to do with children, parents, friends of children, ay, and children themselves. This is the meaning of those words of our Lord, when on this same occasion He said, ' Whoso shall offend one of these little ones, it were better that a millstone were hanged about his neck, and that he were drowned in the depths of the sea.' Think what it is to mislead, or to pervert, or to corrupt, or to give needless pain to any of these children, who were sent to us with the special view of keeping alive within us whatever there is of good or pure or just. An ancient heathen poet has said, ' There is nothing which demands greater reverence at our hands than the conscience of a little boy : '

Maxima debetur pueris reverentia.

To accustom them in their early years to sounds or

sights of cruelty or vice, to teach them by precept or words those bad habits, those slang, vulgar words, which confuse their delicate sense of right or wrong, which deprave their taste for what is beautiful; to encourage, by foolish laughter or by reckless indulgence, the tricks or the mistakes or the frivolities of those who soon learn to know what it is that amuses their elders, and who have a fatal facility of imitating what is bad as well as what is good; these are so many ways of offending God's little ones, causing them to stumble, go astray, spoiling them (to use that homely but most expressive word) for any good word or work in after-life. And, on the other hand, how much can be done to develop, to unfold, to enlighten them from the very first! They are to us the types and likenesses of the whole human race—of religion itself. Every generation is bound to contribute what it can to the formation of that perfect man which is to grow up into the fulness of the stature of Jesus Christ. And so every parent, every teacher, is bound to pour all the light and knowledge and grace that he can into the souls, the eager receptive souls, of those who will grow up to take our place when we are dead and gone. 'Take heed that ye despise not one of these little ones.' No, indeed, they are not to be despised, they have in them the future of the world. 'Their angels,' as the Saviour says, 'behold the face of My Father which is in heaven.' That is to say, their immortal destinies are treasured up in the eternal councils of Providence, as the means by which the world shall be regenerated. That little child which the Saviour held in His arms was, according to the tradition, to grow up to be the future martyr of the early church, Ignatius, the heroic Bishop of Antioch. The children of England at this moment—who knows what may be the lot of any one of them? We remember the mournful regret of the poet in the country churchyard at the thought how there might there be mouldering—

> Hands that the rod of empire might have swayed,
> Or waked to ecstasy the living lyre ;

how

> Some mute inglorious Milton here may rest,
> Some Cromwell guiltless of his country's blood.

But the same thing may occur to any thoughtful man, as he looks over an assembly of children, not with useless regret at what might have been and is not, but with inspiring hope at what may be, and perhaps shall be. They are the rising generation ; they contain the poets, the scholars, the discoverers, the statesmen, the Christians of the future. Their guardian angels, their ideals (so to speak), are at this moment contemplating, in the face of the Eternal Father, the possible destinies of glory, of grace, or of goodness which they may accomplish, and which need only our helping hands to enable them to help themselves, and reach forward to the prize of the high calling of God in Christ Jesus.

And in this, you, my dear children, can take your part. I have hitherto spoken more to your friends and your parents than to you, but you will have heard what I have been saying, and you will feel how great a blessing you can be to them and to all of us if you are good, sweet-tempered, and kind ; and how great a misery if you are naughty, cross, selfish. If you look at the face of your father or mother, your uncle or aunt, or your tutor, you will often seen a dark shade come over it, as if they had some very bad news ; and what do you think it is? It is because they have seen something in you that has distressed them, that has made them fear that you are not going on as you ought, that you have been unkind, or untruthful, or rough. Oh ! drive away that dark shade from their faces, for you only can do it ; you love them, and you would not make them unhappy. And have you not also seen their faces sometimes shine with joy, and their eyes sparkle? and even if they are ill or suffering, have you not seen them cheered up, and seem, for the moment, almost well? Why is it? What has helped them? Have they had a great treasure sent to them? Has a good fairy given them some beautiful palace or kingdom? No. I will tell you what it is. They have heard, they have seen, that their child is going on as they would wish; that their little son or their little nephew shows himself more manly, more attentive to his lessons, more courageous, more kind to dumb creatures, more thoughtful for his brothers and sisters; or that their little daughter or their little niece is growing up more modest, more willing to help her father and mother, more gentle, more compassionate; less thinking of herself, and more of those about her. And can you not also help each other? For it is not only parents that sometimes spoil their children, it is sometimes children who spoil one another. And it is not only parents and teachers who educate and teach their children, it is children who educate and teach one another. Even in the nursery you can keep quiet whilst your little brother and sister are saying their prayers. By giving or keeping back your playthings you can make one another happy or miserable. And as you grow older—you little boys especially, when you go to school—you can be like guardian angels to those who are weaker and younger than you. You can watch over them. You can encourage them in telling the truth, and in keeping from bad words. You can prevent others from teasing them; and when you grow to be men, you will find, perhaps, that the good which you have done to them has never been forgotten; and when some one presses your hand more warmly, or looks gratefully in your face, it will be because he remembers the kindness you did to him when you both sat side by side on the same bench, or played together in the same playground at school. And if any good thought has been put into your hearts to-day, do not let it pass away. Remember that each of you may grow up to be a light in the world, beloved by all good men there, as you are beloved by your brothers and sisters and playfellows. It is told of one recently buried in this Abbey—David Livingstone—that he began to improve himself quite as a young boy in Scotland, reading his books at any odd moment, amidst all the noise and clatter around him when he was at his work; and he ended his life by having made himself so honoured and beloved by the Africans amongst whom he died, that they carried his dead body through every kind of difficulty and danger, till at last it was laid where you see his name and his fame inscribed for ever. And remember that Jesus Christ Himself, the great and good Saviour, began as a child like you. A good man,[1] whose monument was erected in this church by one [2] who loved his poetry dearly, and who is himself departed from us, was always thinking of little children and writing verses for them, and of the love which Jesus Christ had for them; and with some of these verses I will end what I have to say.

> Was not our Lord a little child,
>   Taught by degrees to pray;
> By father dear and mother mild
>   Instructed day by day?
>
> And loved He not of heaven to talk
>   With children in His sight;
> To meet them in His daily walk,
>   And to His arms invite?

In His arms may you all remain to the end of your lives.

[1] Keble.   [2] Edward Twisleton.

IV

THE 'GOLIATH' BOYS.

(December 28, 1875.)

There remaineth yet the youngest, and, behold, he keepeth the sheep.—1 SAM. xvi. 11.

I PROPOSE to set before you to-day an example of what may be expected from children, from little boys, from little girls, when they are quite young; to show you how they may do and say things which will be of the greatest use to those about them, and which will do the greatest good to their own characters. Sometimes we think that they can only do very little, but I will show you that they can do a great deal. Look at David: when Samuel first came to his father's house and asked to see the sons, they came one after another, tall, grown-up men; no one thought of the little boy who was with the sheep. When the huge giant, Goliath of Gath, defied the armies of Israel, he looked round disdainfully, as though he saw no one. But running across the valley there came to the Philistine giant this young boy, with his bright auburn hair, and his fierce quick eyes, and his little satchel round his neck, and his little switch in his hand, with which he kept the sheep-dogs in order. It was he who had sung his songs on the hill-side, where he saw the sun and moon and stars. It was he who had had the courage to run after the lion and the bear, and snatch his sheep or his lambs out of their mouths. It was he who, though his tall brothers thought nothing of him, and the proud Philistine treated him as a mere child, yet was able to do for his country what no one else could do, and with his sling and his stone, with his fleet feet, and his certain aim, and his strong faith, and his undaunted spirit, to overthrow his gigantic enemy. This is a story which is often repeated. It has been repeated in the example of some of the early martyrs ; not only of those children who are commemorated to-day as the Innocent Babes whom Herod killed, and who died not knowing how or why, but later in the history of the Church ; as in the cases of the little boy Pancratius, who is believed to have been a martyr at fourteen, and of the little girl Agnes, who is supposed to have been a martyr at thirteen. There have been some of our own good young princes who are buried in this Abbey. There was that wonderfully gifted boy, Edward VI., who was only sixteen when he died, and who before that time had by his diligence and his honesty made himself beloved and trusted by all about him, and who even had the firmness to resist doing a very cruel act when urged to it by a much older man, who should have known better. There is the good Prince Henry, eldest son of King James I., who when his foolish attendants provoked him to swear because a butcher's dog had killed a stag that he was hunting, said, 'Away with you! all the pleasure in the world is not worth a profane oath.' There was, again, that other Henry, Duke of Gloucester, who sat on the knees of his father, Charles I., on the day before his execution, and who, when his father said to him, 'They will try to make you king instead of your elder brother,' fired up like a little man, and said, 'I will be torn in pieces first.' Well might all these princes be mourned, and have a place in English history, and a place in this Abbey; because, though they died early, they showed of what stuff they were made, and that they would have been fit to be kings, and to be with kings, because they had wills and consciences of their own; because they were afraid of nothing except doing wrong; because they cared for nothing so much as doing their duty.

But perhaps some of you, or of your parents and friends who have the charge of you, will say: 'Oh, but these were young princes, with all the advantages which a great education could give; or, these were martyrs who lived long ago, when times were so different; or, that bright-eyed, light-haired boy, the youthful David, was inspired by God's especial grace to do and say great things, which could not be expected of us.'

But now let me give you an example which comes nearer home. I will speak to you of what has been done by little boys of seven, of eight, of twelve, of thirteen, as young as the youngest of you; little English boys, and English boys with very few advantages of birth, not brought up as most of you are, in quiet, orderly homes, but taken from rough workhouses. I will speak to you of what such little boys have done, not three thousand, or fifteen hundred, or two hundred years ago, but last week—last Wednesday[1]—on this very river Thames. Do you know what I am thinking of? It is of the little boys who were brought

[1] December 22, 1875.

from different workhouses in London, nearly five hundred, and were put to school to be trained as sailors on board the ship which was called after the name of the giant whom David slew—the training-ship *Goliath*, down the Thames. This great ship suddenly, about eight o'clock on Wednesday morning, caught fire. It was hardly light; one of these dark winter mornings when we can hardly see to dress ourselves. In three minutes the ship was on fire from one end to the other, and the fire-bell rang to call the boys each to his post. What did they do? Think of the sudden surprise, the sudden danger, the flames rushing all round them, and the dark cold water below them. Did they cry, or scream, or run, or fly about in confusion? No, they ran each to his proper place; they had been trained to do it; they knew it was their duty, and no one forgot himself, none lost his presence of mind. They all, as the captain says, 'behaved like men.' Then, when it was found impossible to save the ship, those who could swim, at the command of the captain, jumped into the water, and swam for their lives. Some at his command got into a boat; and then, when the sheets of flame and clouds of smoke came pouring out of the ship upon them, the smaller boys for a moment were frightened, and wanted to push away. But there was one among them—the little mate—his name was William Bolton. We are proud here that he came from Westminster. A quiet boy, they tell us, and one much loved by his comrades. He had the sense and the courage to say, 'No; we must stay and help those that are still in the ship.' He kept the barge alongside of the ship as long as possible, and was thus the means of saving more than one hundred lives. And there were others, who were still in the ship while the flames went on spreading, and they came and stood by the good captain who had been so kind to them all, and whom they all loved so much; and in that dreadful moment they thought more of him than of themselves; and one threw his arms round his neck, and said, 'You'll be burnt, captain:' and another said, 'Save yourself before the rest.' But the captain gave them the best of all lessons at that moment; he said, 'That's not the way at sea, my boys.' He meant to say—and they quite understood what he meant—that the way at sea is to prepare for danger beforehand, to meet it manfully when it comes, and to look at the safety not of oneself, but of others. 'And thus,' as says the public journal in speaking of it, 'the captain not only had learned that good old way himself, but knew how to teach it to the boys under his charge.'

And now let me ask you to consider what we may all learn from this story of the good conduct of the boys in the *Goliath* ship. First, what an encouragement it is to parents, teachers, nurses, all who do anything for children, as showing that their labour is not spent in vain! These little boys were taken from a rough, neglected class, which had before been a trouble and vexation to all about them. By the foresight and energy of the Minister of State who began this system of training-ships, and then by the constant, genial, wise kindness of the captain and his wife and daughters, always having a kind word and look for these little boys, making them feel their ship to be their home, instructing them in habits of order and duty and religion, they were being trained to be the servants of their country and their God in that noble profession of an English sailor. And now that they have been suddenly put on their trial in this great calamity, we see how all this had told upon them. What seeds of goodness were there in these little hearts! what energy given to those little minds! This is what education can do; this is what can be done by making a good beginning. I know, we all know, that good beginnings may have bad endings; that these little heroes, as we may call them, of the *Goliath* ship may, if they are spoiled by foolish flattery, or meet with wicked companions, turn out very differently from what they are now. There has been a dreadful example, within the last month, of one who began as a charming, enterprising, intelligent, religious boy, but who, from giving way to evil courses and bad associates, ended in committing a frightful crime, and died last week, with the infamy of a selfish, hard-hearted murderer.[2] But these things are the exceptions. Let us hope and believe that whenever care, forethought, and kindness are exerted on young children, they will lead the rest of their lives according to that good beginning. It is the best we can do for them; it is the best we can do for our country.

And you, children, turn your thoughts once again back to that burning ship, and the example of the little boys all doing their duty so nobly. What is it that this teaches you? It teaches you that you ought to be always ready to do what is right at a moment's notice. These boys could never have guessed, when they got up on the

[2] Wainwright.

morning of that day, that in three minutes they would have to be all working to save their lives, and the lives of those about them. But they were ready, and they did it. There is a fine old motto of an old Scottish family, 'Ready, aye ready': let that be your motto. When a sudden alarm comes—perhaps fire in the middle of the night, perhaps some other danger—try to keep what is called presence of mind; do not run about here and there, as if you had lost your senses, but be quiet, be calm. Do what you are bid, and you may save father, mother, brothers, and sisters. And again, when a sudden temptation comes upon you to go after what is wrong, saying foolish, filthy words, or telling a lie, or over-eating yourselves, or being unkind, remember those boys in the *Goliath*. They stood firm to what they knew was their duty. They stood firm though the flames were raging round them; they were like the three children in the midst of the burning fiery furnace, who were as true to their conscience, and as calm, as though the fire had been a moist whistling wind. And remember how, when those who were in the boat were a moment dismayed, there was one, the little mate, who had the courage to persist in keeping close to the ship, and so saved many,

many of his dear friends. Be like that little mate: when you are pressed to do anything wrong, have the boldness to say No. A very wise man has said that any one who has learnt to say *No* has made the first step to being a good, useful, great man. Do not care how many there may be against you; do not think of the trouble of doing right. Do it, and take the consequences. Even if the burning masts had fallen upon the *Goliath* boys and killed them all, it would have been better for them all to have died in that way, and be buried by the little boy who is this day laid to rest in the village church of Grays, than that they should have weakly given way, and shown the white feather, or failed in one atom of their duty. And think what a reward, what an exceeding great reward, you give to your parents and your teachers by any such good conduct. When that little boy clasped his arms round the captain's neck, and begged him to go, and said, 'You'll be burnt, captain, if you stay,' do not you think that that moment must have made up to the captain for all the trouble and pains he had spent on these boys, to see that they loved him, and would have given their lives for him? Remember that short speech of the captain when they asked him to leave the ship: "That's not the way at sea, my boys.' That is the best advice for all of us. We are all on our voyage through life, over many waves of this troublesome world. There is one way of getting out of these troubles—it is by selfishly thinking of ourselves, by leaving our companions in the wood, by taking the best for ourselves, by avoiding risk and danger and pain, and seeking our own profit and pleasure. This is what is done by many children, and by many men. 'But that is not the way at sea, my boys.' It is the way of the world. It is the way of cowards, and spendthrifts, and spoiled children, and selfish men; but it is not the way of English sailors, it is not the way of Christian Englishmen, it is not the way to noble lives and glorious deaths. There 'is the way at sea'—the way of standing by your post till the last, doing your duty whatever comes, thinking more of others than of yourself, jumping into the face of danger rather than flying away in dishonour, working away quietly and calmly and manfully to do as much good as you can whilst life is granted to you. 'That's the way at sea, my boys.' That was the way of the boys in the burning ship. That is the way in which England's sailors, like Commodore Goodenough, have won for themselves an immortal name. That is the way of good children, honourable boys, and gallant men; the way of Christian heroes and Christian martyrs That is the way in which we trust that this day will teach you to walk henceforth, and till the latest day of your lives.

V.

THE CHILDREN'S PSALMS.

(December 28, 1876.)

Out of the mouth of babes and sucklings hast Thou ordained strength.—Ps. viii. 2. *Like as the arrows in the hand of the giant, even so are the young children.*—Ps. cxxvii. 5 (Prayer Book version). *Lord, who shall abide in Thy tabernacle? who shall dwell in Thy holy hill?*—Ps. xv. 1.

WHEN, year by year, we see a congregation of children with their parents assembled, it is, or ought to be, a joy and comfort to those who feel the burden of life, the darkening shades of sorrow, and the weight of care. Why is this? Why is the sight of children a consolation? Parents, perhaps, will understand best what I have to say at first, although I shall also have to say something which children will understand for themselves. I have taken these verses from the three Psalms which are sung on occasion of these gatherings to express what I mean.

I. The first is from the eighth Psalm. That is

a Psalm which almost certainly was written by David. He wishes to unravel his thoughts, and to have a clear idea of God; and he finds it in two things; in the moon and the stars, which we see in the sky on a cloudless night, and which cause him to think of the order with which this great universe has been arranged; and in the bright faces and the blameless talk of little children. Little children give him an idea of what man, who was born in the image of God, was meant to be. No doubt there are bad children, naughty children; and even in good children there is something which may become very bad. Still, in children there is an innocence, a lightness of heart, an ignorance of evil, a joyousness, and a simplicity, which ought to be refreshing to every one. It was this which made our Saviour so fond of them—taking them up in His arms and saying, 'Of such is the kingdom of heaven;' and it is this which is well expressed by a good English poet, who says, as he looks back regretfully to his childhood—

>Happy those early days when I
>Shined in my angel infancy;
>. . . . . .
>Before I taught my tongue to wound
>My conscience with a sinful sound;
>. . . . . .

> But felt through all this fleshly dress
> Bright shoots of everlastingness.
> Oh, how I long to travel back,
> And tread again that ancient track![1]

And this it is, also, which gives a soothing thought to any who have lost their darlings in infancy or in early childhood. Their lives were complete. They had shown us the glory of God in their dear little ways. They have gone to be with Him. 'We reckon not by years and months where they have gone to dwell.' May I read to you the words of a great scholar and philosopher[2] after the death of a sweet daughter? Parents may take the words to themselves, and children may know from them what a comfort they may be for their parents if they have been good and gentle and diligent. 'As soon as her last breath was gone I was able to thank God that He had taken my child into His arms, where she is safe for ever from all the troubles and the sorrows of life. The first chapter of her existence has closed. Who knows what troubles might have been in store for her? But she was found worthy to enter the kingdom of heaven as a little child. Here we have toiled for many years, and been troubled with many questionings, but

---

[1] Henry Vaughan, *The Retreat*.   [2] Max Müller.

what is the end of it all? We must learn to become simple again like little children. That is all we have a right to be; for this life was meant to be the childhood of our souls, and the more we try to be what we were meant to be, the better for us. Let us use the powers of our minds with the greatest freedom and love of truth; but let us never forget that we are, as Newton said, "like children playing on the sea-shore, while the great ocean of truth lies undiscovered before us."

II. But we must not, in thinking of children, think only of them in the past. We must think of their future; and here let us look at another Psalm, the hundred and twenty-seventh, a Psalm which some of the Jewish teachers long ago thought might have been written by the great King Solomon. At any rate, it expresses what a man of vast experience of human life might well have said. It tells us that we must console ourselves in the sorrows and troubles of the present time by thinking of what the children who stand around us may be in the time which is coming. They are like the arrows which a mighty archer can shoot far away into the distance and the darkness, and so strike a target which we, perhaps, can hardly see, but which, if these little arrows are winged with good thoughts, and pointed with good resolves, and polished by a good training, they will surely reach. We may sometimes, as we look towards the immediate future of our country, think sadly perhaps how few great characters or glorious gifts there are to enlighten the close of this nineteenth century, as we and our fathers were enlightened by the great characters and the glorious gifts of those who adorned its beginning. But our consolation may be that those who are the children of this generation shall grow up to fill this void, and to comfort those who are still unborn. Amongst the children who are now present here, there must be many who will live to the twentieth century. Let them remember, when the first year of the next century shall dawn upon them, that they were called upon, as now in this Abbey, to take their part in rendering their country a great, a happy, and a Christian nation. Where we have failed, let them succeed; where we have succeeded, let them improve; where we have lost, let them recover. Happy is that country which has its quiver full of good, strong, active, honest, Christian children. She shall not be afraid when she speaks with her enemies in the gate. There is a long, long day before many of you. Make the very most of it. Let us feel assured that when we die and pass away we shall have left our country, our religion, and our honour, safe in your hands.

III. And this brings me to the third lesson which we may take from these Psalms. The fifteenth Psalm also is almost certainly written by David. It was what he wrote, we may suppose, when he had conquered Jerusalem, and asked who was worthy to live in the holy city; that is, what are the characters that God loves and wishes to be with Him? There is no difficulty in understanding what David says in the verses which follow the first; and when people talk of the difficulty of teaching religion to children, let them remember these verses of the fifteenth Psalm. They will find how very easily they can be learned, and how very easily they can be applied. I will try to apply them now; and so I turn to you, my children, and having told you how much we and your country expect from you, I will tell you who it is that shall be thought worthy of the house of God and His holy hill; and I will ask those who are parents and friends, or who have any influence over any of these children, to try to make a good atmosphere round about them, so that these conditions may become possible and easy for them. What, then, is it that we may recommend to all children if they would wish to please their parents, to please God, and to go to heaven? Love honest work. Love to get knowledge. Never forget to say your prayers morning and evening, never be ashamed to say them. It will help you to be good all through the day. Always keep your promises. Do not pick up foolish and dirty stories. Never, never tell a lie. Never strike, or hurt, or be rude to a woman or a girl, or to any one weaker or younger than yourselves. Be ready even to risk your own lives to save a friend, or a companion, or a brother, or a sister. Be very kind to poor dumb animals. Never put them to pain. They are God's creatures as well as you; and if you hurt them you will become brutal and base yourselves. Remember always to be gentle and attentive to older people. Listen, and do not interrupt when they are talking. If you have an old father or grandfather, or a sick uncle or aunt, remember not to disturb them by loud talking or rough playing. Be careful and tender to them. You cannot think what good it does them. And if it should happen that any amongst you have poor fathers or poor mothers who have to get up early in order to go about their business, and to earn their bread and your bread, remember what a pleasure it will be to them to find that their little boy or their little girl has been out of bed before them on a cold winter morning, and lighted a bright, blazing fire, so as to give them a warm cup of tea. Think what pleasure it will be to them if they are sick, or if they are deaf, or if they are blind, to find a little boy or a little girl to speak to them, to read to them, and to lead them about. But there is not only the comfort which is experienced in being thus helped; there is the still greater comfort of knowing that they have a good little son or a good little daughter who is anxious to assist them, and who, they feel sure, will be a joy, and not a trouble to them, by day and by night. No Christmas present can be so welcome to any father and mother as the belief that their children are growing up truthful, manly, courageous, courteous, unselfish, and religious. And do not think that any of these things are too much for any of you. I know that many of you have great temptations. Perhaps you may have homes where it is very difficult to be tidy and clean. Perhaps, as you go to school along the streets, there may be wicked people who endeavour to lead you astray, and who try to make you steal, and use bad words. Yet I am sure that, if you do your best, you will find such delight in doing your duty that you will go on in what is good. Let the good frighten the bad; let the light drive away the darkness; let the whole world know that there are little English boys and girls who are determined to do their duty whatever befalls them. Some of you may remember that, last year, I spoke of the gallant boys who behaved so well on board the *Goliath* ship when it was on fire. Well, these same boys have just begun their training over again. It was only on Tuesday last that they got on board their new ship, the *Exmouth*; and there they are working for their country once more. God bless and prosper them, and may they still be examples to all of us. It was only the other day, also, that I heard of a brave, modest little boy—Hammond Parker was his name—who was only just fourteen years of age, but who had saved, at different times, the lives of no fewer than four other boys by plunging into the rough sea after them on the coast of Norfolk. Now, that shows what you may all do—not, perhaps, by plunging into the stormy sea, but, at any rate, by saving little brothers or little sisters from going wrong. You can do far more for them than, perhaps, any one else, because you are always with them. Stand by them, protect them;

stand by each other; and then the foolish, wicked, and cruel people who want to mislead you will very soon run away. Bad people are almost always afraid of good people, even though the good are much fewer; even, indeed, though the good may be only a little child. I knew once a very famous man (it was Adam Sedgwick), who lived to be eighty-eight years old, and who was the delight of every one about him. He always stood up for what was right. His eye was like the eagle's when it flashed fire against what was wrong. And how early do you think he began to do this? I have an old grammar which belonged to him, all tattered and torn, which he had when he was a little boy at school; and what do I find written in his own hand on the first page of it? I find these words from Shakespeare: 'Still in thy right hand carry gentle peace, to silence envious tongues. Be just and fear not.' That was his rule all through life, and he was loved and honoured down to the day when he was borne to his grave. Be just, be good, and fear not. Let that be your rule; and God and Jesus Christ will be with you now and always.

VI.

SICK CHILDREN.

(December 28, 1877.)

Is it well with the child? . . . It is well.[1]— 2 KINGS iv. 26.

I HAVE usually spoken to you on this day of the life and happiness of children. I wish to speak to you this evening of the sufferings and sorrows of children, and concerning children—or rather, I will say, of the happiness which out of their sufferings and sorrows God intends to bring to us.

First let me speak of the death of children. It is one of the chief thoughts placed before us by the Festival of the *Innocents*—the Holy Innocents, as they are called. We know nothing about those little children of Bethlehem, except that they died. What is the good which can be brought to any of

---

[1] I have been reminded that a sermon on this text was preached by Dr. Doddridge on the death of a beloved child, the words having been written actually on the child's coffin.

us, old or young, by the death of those dear little ones, who had been lent to us for so short a time that we seem to have lost them almost before we have time to know them? 'Is it well with the child?' said Elisha to the mother of the little boy that he had known from his birth. The little boy was dead; but the poor mother was still able to say, 'It is well.' Yes, there are several ways in which, even in this hard trial, we may say, 'It is well.' 'It is well,' because in God's sight all that happens is well, if only we use it rightly. 'It is well,' because the child that dies in its innocence is taken, if any human creature is, to the presence of God and of Jesus Christ. He Himself has told us that the characters of little children are the likeness of the characters in heaven. When we think of heaven we think of them. 'It is well,' because it makes, or ought to make, on our hearts an impression which perhaps nothing else can make. Even a hard-hearted man, when his child dies, or his little brother dies, is deeply moved. He thinks that he might have been more kind whilst they lived. He looks at the little vacant chair, and his eyes fill with tears.

And we are comforted by thinking of them.

I have heard of a little child dying with such

bright and beautiful visions before him that his countenance was quite transfigured, and glowed as with heavenly colours; and his parents, as they looked at him, were more than consoled. They went away strengthened in their faith and hopeful in their good deeds.

This Abbey is full of the remembrances of great men and famous women. But it is also full of the remembrances of little boys and girls whose death shot a pang through the hearts of those who loved them, and who wished that they never should be forgotten.

Almost the earliest royal monument in this Abbey is of a beautiful little deaf and dumb girl of five years old—the Princess Catherine, daughter of King Henry III., who loved her dearly. She has not been forgotten, nor have her two little brothers, and perhaps four little nephews, who were buried close to her, as if to keep her company. And so there are two small tombs in Henry VII.'s chapel of the two infant daughters of King James I. Over one of them are some touching lines written by an American lady, which all mothers should read. And to these tombs of these two little girls were brought in after days by their nephew, Charles II., the bones of the two young murdered princes, which in his time were discovered at the foot of the staircase in the Tower.

And there is in the chapel of St. Nicholas another tomb of a little child that died from a mistake of its nurse; and we know [2] from her will that she never ceased to lament the little darling, and begged very urgently, if possible, to be buried beside it. And there is in the cloisters the monument mentioned on a previous occasion,[3] which contains only these words, 'Jane Lister, dear child,' with the date and the record of her brother's previous death. It is an inscription which goes to the heart of every one. It was in the year 1688, just a month before the great English Revolution, but the parents thought only of 'Jane Lister,' their 'dear child.'

Do not forget the dead children. They are not forgotten in Westminster Abbey, they ought never to be forgotten elsewhere. Mothers, parents, who, like Rachel, mourn for some dear daughter or son, think that they are still yours, to animate and urge you forwards. That was a true answer which the little girl made to the poet Wordsworth, who asked how many they were—

---

[2] Colonel Chester's edition of *The Registers of Westminster Abbey*, p. 220. [3] See p. 20.

> 'Seven boys and girls are we;
> Two of us in the churchyard lie,
> Beneath the churchyard tree.'
>
> 'How many are you then?' said I,
> 'If they two are in heaven?'
> Quick was the little Maid's reply,
> 'O Master, we are seven!'

And there is another beautiful poem by the father of three sons : [4] two were living, but the third was dead. Of him he thus speaks :—

> I have a son—a third sweet son ; his age I cannot tell,
> For they reckon not by years and months where he is gone to dwell. . . .
> I cannot tell what form is his, what look he weareth now,
> Nor guess how bright a glory crowns his shining seraph brow. . . .
> But I know, for God doth tell me this, that he is now at rest,
> Where other blessed infants be, on their Saviour's loving breast. . . .
> Whate'er befall his brethren twain, his bliss can never cease ;
> Their lot may here be grief and fear, but his is certain peace.

But I would not speak only of dead children. I will speak of sick children, of children who have some illness or infirmity, crippled, or weak, or ailing, like some of those who are here to-day from

[4] Moultrie's poem on 'The Three Sons.'

the Royal Infirmary for Children. '*Is it well*' with those suffering little ones? Yes, 'it is well,' for them and for us, if we take the sickness as it is intended by our heavenly Father.

There is a beautiful picture, by the famous painter Holbein, of a family who are praying, or perhaps giving thanks, for the recovery of their sick child; and the prayer is supposed to be granted by the appearance of the child Jesus in the midst of the family, happy and strong, whilst the poor sickly child is represented as in the arms of the Virgin Mother, taken as her own. That is a likeness to us of what we ought to hope for in the case of our sick and ailing children. The sickness may perhaps continue, but the sufferer may be under the protection of our good Father, and nursed as it were for Himself; and amongst us the child, the inner spirit of the child, which will grow up amidst suffering and weakness, is like the spirit of the holy child Jesus, happy and strong, and pure and good.

Sickness and illness may make a child fretful and selfish, and the people about a sick child may spoil it by giving up everything to it, and encouraging it to ask for everything. But it may also teach a child to be patient and considerate, and grateful for all the care it gets; and then, instead of being a source of sorrow and vexation in the household, it becomes a source of instruction and comfort to all.

I will try to make this clear to you from several examples. One is taken from a story: it is one which some of you may have read, called the 'Heir of Redclyffe.' In that story is described a sickly boy called Charles. He is, at the beginning of the story, like one of those fretful, peevish invalids of whom I spoke just now; speaking sharply and crossly to every one, and making every one's will bend to his. But in the course of the story there comes into the house another boy full of health and life, but also full of generosity and kindness, and the sickly, selfish boy turns over a new leaf; his character is transformed as the story goes on. He still remains a suffering cripple, but he becomes the stay and support of the house; instead of always demanding comfort from them, he, in all the troubles of the family, gives comfort to all the others.

This is from a story, an imaginary tale of what might happen. Now I will tell you of what has happened. It is a contrast between two boys in Scotland, to which my attention was called some time ago by an excellent Scottish judge, now dead.[5] They were boys who both became famous in after life, and many of you have heard of their names. One was Lord Byron, the other was Sir Walter Scott. Well, both these boys had the same kind of misfortune. Both Lord Byron and Walter Scott, from their earliest years, were lame. Each of them had what is called a club foot, or something very like it. But now what was the different effect produced by this lame foot on the two boys? Lord Byron, who was a perverse, selfish boy, was made by this club foot discontented and angry with every one about him. It entered like iron into his soul. It poisoned his heart. It set him against all mankind, and it injured his whole character. He had a splendid genius, but amidst many fine qualities it was a genius blackened and discoloured by hatred, malice, uncharitableness, and the deepest gloom. Walter Scott, on the other hand, never lost his cheerfulness. His lame foot made him turn to the reading of good old books, and to the enjoyment of the beautiful sights and sounds about him, and he too grew to be a great poet and the writer of stories which will live in every age and in every country. But in him the lameness which he had

[5] Lord Neaves.

borne patiently and cheerfully in childhood never interfered with his kindliness and his good-humour to those about him. He was a delight to all that came across him, and even when he was at last overtaken by heavier misfortunes he never lost his loving, generous disposition. The lameness which in Byron turned to what St. Paul calls a savour of death unto death, became in Walter Scott a savour of life unto life.

This, then, is the lesson which I would wish to teach to all children who are sickly and suffering, or who may become sickly and suffering: Do not think that you are without an object, do not think that you cannot be useful, do not think that everything has gone against you. No. It is well with you: you can be most useful, you can be *the* useful child; and when you grow up you can be *the* useful man or *the* useful woman in the home. You can arrange plans of amusement for the others who are too busy to arrange them for themselves. You can show by your constant cheerfulness that happiness does not depend on the good things which you eat, or on the active games which you play, but on a contented, joyful heart. You can make them feel that there is a better world above, where you hope to be, and where you may be almost now, because your thoughts are with God and with Jesus Christ. And you children who are strong and healthy, remember that to you this little sick brother or little sick sister is a blessing that God has given you. *It is well* for you to have them. They may not be able to share in your games; you will often be obliged to be quiet in their sick room, or when they come amongst you. But that is good for you, because it makes you see very early the joy, the happiness, the usefulness, of having some one weaker than yourselves whom you can protect; some one in pain or suffering to whom you can minister like a ministering angel. Do not be hasty or angry with a deaf brother, or I may say a deaf mother or aunt, because they cannot hear you; or a blind sister, or I may say a blind father or uncle, because they cannot see you; or with a lame or deformed brother or cousin or companion, because they cannot take an active part in your amusements. No. They cannot do this: but they can do much better than this for you, because they make you feel for deafness and blindness and lameness everywhere. When you have seen it in those you love, you will be reminded of it in those you do not love.

And if you have had any of these misfortunes

yourselves, and have grown out of them, the recollection of what you have suffered may make you of much use to others. There is a distinguished man, very high in rank, and of absolutely indispensable value in the public service of his Church and country, who when a little boy was very lame.[6] He recovered, but he never lost his fellow-feeling for lame people; and once, when we were walking together, I remember that he gave some money to a poor lame man who opened the gate for us, and he told me that he always did so, in remembrance of his own lameness.

Learn to be tender to your suffering brothers or sisters. You who are sick or weakly, always keep up that fellow-feeling. It will make your weakness or illness a blessing, and not a curse. You who are well and have sick friends, you also try to keep up that fellow-feeling. In the story of Elisha and the sick child, we are told that when he hoped to restore the child to health 'he went up and lay upon the child, and put his mouth upon the child's mouth, and his eyes upon the child's eyes, and his hands upon the child's hands; and he stretched himself upon the child,' and the flesh of the child waxed warm. This is a likeness of the sym-

[6] Archbishop Tait.

pathy which all in health, whether old or young, should try to have for those who are in pain or infirmity. We give life and happiness to the sick by giving them, as it were, a taste of our life and happiness; our words are words to them, our eyes are eyes to them, our hands are hands to them. There were some sailors who were stranded on a desert rock on a freezing night. There was one little midshipman amongst them; they put their clothes upon him, they covered him up. They all were found dead in the morning; but, if I remember right, the little boy, through their kindness, survived—their warmth had saved him, they died that he might live. And so, even without such great efforts, we should try to put ourselves in the place of our sick and suffering companions. We should try to feel for them, as we should wish them to feel for us, to tell them of the happy and beautiful things of the outside world, to make them understand that they are not forgotten, to show them what is the sphere in which they can be useful.

It is for this reason that hospitals for sick children are so much to be encouraged. In old barbarous heathen times the life of a sick or deformed child was not thought worth preserving. The sickly children were thrown on the road as not worth saving. But they *are* worth saving; they may be the saving of those about them. One of the first great changes that were made by Christianity was that those sick children left to perish were adopted by kind men and women, who brought them up as their own. And so not only in hospitals, but in every family where there is a sick child, remember that it is your duty, your privilege, to look after such. If you are kind to them God will be kind to you. They are your special charges; they are the good things committed by God to us for our keeping. They are our earliest and best teachers in the good way. Whoever does anything for them does it to the good God and merciful Saviour who entrusted them to us. And we shall not lose our reward. *It will be well* for the children and *it will be well* for us.

VII.

ST. CHRISTOPHER.

(December 28, 1878.)

Like as the arrows in the hand of the giant, even so are the young children. Ps. cxxvii. 5.

THERE is an old story, a kind of Sunday fairy tale, which you may sometimes have seen represented in pictures and statues in ancient churches (there are two sculptures of it in King Henry VII.'s chapel in this church), of a great heathen giant who wished to find out some master that he should think worthy of his service, some one stronger than himself. He went about the world, but could find no one stronger. And besides this, he was anxious to pray to God, but did not know how to do it. At last he met with a good old man by the side of a deep river, where poor wayfaring people wanted to get across, and had no one to help them. And the good old man said to the giant, 'Here is a place where you can be of some use; and if you do not know how to pray, you will, at any rate, know how to work, and perhaps God will give you what you ask, and perhaps also you will at last find a master stronger than you.' So the giant went and sat by the river-side, and many a time he carried poor wayfarers across. One night he heard a little child crying to be carried over; so he put the child on his shoulder and strode across the stream. Presently the wind blew, the rain fell, and as the river beat against his knees he felt the weight of the little child almost greater than he could bear, and he looked up with his great, patient eyes (there is a beautiful picture in a beautiful palace at Venice, where we see him with his face turned upwards as he tries to steady himself in the raging waters), and he saw that it was a child glorious and shining; and the child said, 'Thou art labouring under this heavy burden because thou art carrying One who bears the sins of all the world.' And then as the story goes on, the giant felt that it was the child Jesus, and when he reached the other side of the river he fell down before Him. Now he had found some one stronger than he was, some one so good, so worthy of loving, as to be a master whom he could serve.

In later days the thought of the giant Christopher (the 'bearer of the child Christ') was so dear to men, that his picture was often painted very large on the churches, so that those who saw it far off should have a pleasant and holy remembrance through the day which would save them from running into evil. But we all may learn from it two useful lessons, which may keep us from evil and lead us into good.

The first lesson is that often, when we know not how to believe or how to pray, we at any rate may know how to work for the good of others, and then God accepts this as if it were a prayer. There is an old Latin saying, *Laborare est orare*—or, if we were to turn it into English, we should say,—

> Good working and good playing
> Is almost like good praying.

Or, as some one else has said,—

> He prayeth well who loveth well
> Both man and bird and beast.

We ought all of us to say our prayers; they will help us to do what is good: but we must also all remember that our prayers are no use unless we strive, both in our work and in our play,

> To live more nearly as we pray.

This is one lesson which we may carry with us from the story of St. Christopher, and one which applies to all, whether grown-up people or children. Pray and work, work and pray, do as much good as you can, and God will reward and receive you at last.

But there is another lesson which more especially applies to the sight of a congregation of children with their parents and friends. The child Jesus, who, according to the story, was carried on the shoulders of the giant, was the type and likeness of all children. That is one reason why we think so much of Christmas; why Christmas is so much more loved than even Easter or Whitsuntide. It is because we feel that the birth and the childhood of our Lord contained the promise of His manhood, because we have our hearts drawn towards the tender, innocent child who, when He grew up, suffered so much and endured so much for the good of mankind. And that may be the case, more or less, with all children. That is why our Saviour looked upon them with such confidence, such reverence, and such affection. 'Of such,' He said, 'is the kingdom of heaven.' Of such and out of such characters as were wrapped up in the little beings which He saw before Him, and which we now see before us, is the hope of the coming time. You who are the parents, you who are responsible for the training of these children, you bear upon your shoulders a burden like that which the giant of the old story carried ; you bear a burden greater, perhaps, than you know how to bear—the burden of forming their characters ; the burden, perchance, of the destinies of the coming age. Rejoice in them, and while remembering how heavy is the responsibility which presses upon you, be encouraged to carry your little burdens safely over the great river of life, which is also the great river of death. Remember also that as St. Christopher in the old story was saved by carrying the Child, so we may be saved by the children carrying us ; they may help by their innocence and truthfulness to teach us now and to help us hereafter ; they may be as that little child which Elisha cured, who it was supposed afterwards grew to be the great prophet Jonah ; or that other little child in the Gospels who, as the early Christians believed, grew to be the great Christian martyr Ignatius.

But as the children are the burden, the quiver on our shoulders, so they are, as the text says, 'like as the arrows in the hand of the giant,' like the arrows which a mighty archer shoots into the darkness, piercing hearts which are far away. These children, if rightly trained and rightly nurtured, may indeed be the blessing of times to come; nay, more, they may be blessings even while they are yet children. Let me give you one simple instance. It is a story, not like that old fairy story with which I began this sermon, but a real story of our own time. I found it in a sermon[1] by a powerful preacher in one of the strange cities of North America, but describing what happened in our own country on a cold winter day like those which we have just had. Listen to it, parents; listen to it, dear children, for if you have understood nothing else of what I have said, you will understand this. Not long ago, in Edinburgh, two gentlemen were standing at the door of an hotel one very cold day, when a little boy with a poor thin blue face, his feet bare and red with the cold, and with nothing to cover him but a bundle of rags, came and said, 'Please, sir, buy some matches.' 'No, I don't want any,' the gentleman said. 'But they are only a penny a box,' the poor little fellow

---

[1] 'The Life that now is:' *Sermons*, by Robert Collyer, of Chicago, pp. 260-64. The story is taken from this volume almost word for word, and I have incorporated some of the preacher's forcible remarks.

pleaded. 'Yes, but you see we don't want a box,' the gentleman said again. 'Then I will gie ye twa boxes for a penny,' the boy said at last; 'and so to get rid of him' (the gentleman who tells the story says) 'I bought a box; but then I found I had no change, so I said, "I will buy a box to-morrow." "Oh, do buy them to-night, if you please," the boy pleaded again; "I will run and get ye the change, for I am verra hungry." So I gave him the shilling, and he started away. I waited for him, but no boy came. Then I thought I had lost my shilling; still there was that in the boy's face I trusted, and I did not like to think ill of him. Late in the evening I was told that a little boy wanted to see me. When he was brought in I found it was a smaller brother of the boy that got my shilling, but if possible still more ragged and poor and thin. He stood a moment, diving into his rags as if he was seeking something, and then said, "Are you the gentleman that bought the matches frae Sandie?" "Yes." "Weel, then, here's fourpence out o' yer shilling; Sandie cannot come; he's very ill; a cart ran ower him and knocked him down, and he lost his bonnet and his matches and your sevenpence, and both his legs are broken, and the doctor says he'll die; and that's a'." And then, putting the fourpence on the table, the poor child broke down into great sobs. So I fed the little man, and I went with him to see Sandie. I found that the two little things lived almost alone, their father and mother being dead. Poor Sandie was lying on a bundle of shavings: he knew me as soon as I came in, and said, " I got the change, sir, and was coming back; and then the horse knocked me down, and both my legs were broken;—and oh, Reuby! little Reuby! I am sure I am dying, and who will take care of you when I am gone? What will ye do, Reuby?" Then I took his hand, and said that I would always take care of Reuby. He understood me, and had just strength to look up at me as if to thank me: the light went out of his blue eyes; in a moment—

> He lay within the light of God,
> Like a babe upon the breast,
> Where the wicked cease from troubling,
> And the weary are at rest.'

That story is like an arrow in the hand of a giant. It ought to pierce many a heart, old and young. Whenever, dear children, you are tempted to say what is not true, or to be hard on other little boys and girls, or to take what you ought not to take, we want you to remember little Sandie. This poor little boy, lying on a bundle of shavings, dying and starving, was tender, and trusty, and true; and so God told the gentleman to take poor little friendless Reuben, and be a friend to him, and Sandie heard him say he would do it—the last thing he ever did hear; and then the dark room, the bundle of shavings, the weary, broken little limbs, all faded away, and Sandie was among the angels, who could look at him in his new home, and say one to another, 'That is the little boy who kept his word, and sent back fourpence; that is the little boy who was tender, and trusty, and true, when he was hungry and faint, and when both his legs were broken, and he lay dying.' This story is told you now because, whether it be hard or easy, we want you to be tender, and trusty, and true, as poor little Sandie, who did not forget his promise, and who loved his little brother to the end.

VIII.

THE CHILDREN'S CREED.

(December 27, 1879.)

I have no greater joy than to hear that my children walk in truth.—3 JOHN 4.

As once before, so now, we have brought you together on St. John's Day, because Innocents' Day falls on a Sunday. Those words which I have read from St. John well express what all of us ought to feel—' We have no greater joy than that our children, than that the rising generation, should walk in truth.' And I have, therefore, thought it useful to set forth what are the religious truths which we should try to teach our children, and which our children should try to learn. Some of what I say will be chiefly addressed to parents and friends; some of what I say will be chiefly addressed to children. But I hope that most will find

—some in one part, some in another—something to instruct them.

There are two points to be mentioned at the outset which might seem difficult to reconcile, but which in fact wonderfully agree, and are a support to each other. On the one hand, what we teach to children should be truths which will stand the wear and tear of time as they grow up. Solomon says, 'Train up a child in the way he should go: and when he is old, he will not depart from it.' That is very true, but in order that he should not depart from it when he is old, it must be a way which, when he is old, he will find to be as good for him as it was when he was young. On the other hand, we must try to teach a child what he will understand, in the simplest and not in the hardest words, in the words which sink deepest into his soul and lay most hold on his heart. This, perhaps we might think, cannot be the truth in which the child will feel most delight when it grows older. Not perhaps in the very same forms; but we may be sure, and our Saviour Himself has told us, that the instruction which is most suitable for a little child is also the most suitable for the oldest and wisest of men.

I. What then shall we teach our children to

believe, which when they grow up they may find that later experience does not require them to alter?

(1) We must teach them that, beyond what they feel and see and touch, there is something better and greater, which they can neither feel nor see nor touch. Goodness, kindness to one another, unselfishness, fairness, and uprightness—these are the best things in all the world. It is true that goodness and kindness have no faces that we can kiss—no hands that we can clasp; but they are certainly close to us, both in the midst of our work and our play. And this goodness and kindness which, except in outward acts, we cannot see, is something which existed before we were born. It is from this that we have all the pleasant things of this world—the flowers, the sunshine, the moonlight—all these were given us by some great kindness and goodness which we have never seen at all. And this Goodness and this Love are the Great Power out of which all things come, which we call by the name of God. And because God is so much above us and so good to us, we call Him by the name which is most dear to us of all earthly names—our Father. When a father goes away from home, still his children know that he is somewhere, though they

cannot see him, and they know what to do in order to please him. So it is with the great unseen Father of us all. Let us then teach our children that God is Goodness and Justice; that the rules which He has laid down for the government of the world are His will and wish for us; even frost and cold, even sickness and pain, are for our good, and we must trust that he has some good reason for it, perhaps to make us strong, and brave, and healthy. It is for this reason that you see in the Abbey, on the monument of Sir John Franklin, who was so long shut up in the ice, the words, 'O ye Frost and Cold; O ye Ice and Snow; bless ye the Lord; praise Him, and magnify Him for ever.' This, then, in various ways, is our way of expressing our belief in our Father in heaven.

(2) But this highest kindness and fairness are like what we have seen and heard of in the world. Children can see it in their good parents, their good uncles and aunts, their good brothers and sisters; and as they grow older they will find that there have always been good people, and they will hear that there was once one Child, one Man, so good to all about Him, so good to little children, that He has shown us better than any one else what is the true likeness of that unseen Goodness which

we call God, and which we still hope to know in heaven. Children should be taught what Jesus Christ did and said when He went about doing good, and should be made to understand that only so far as we are like to Jesus Christ, or like what Jesus Christ loved when He was in the world, can we be His friends or followers. He was good, and He went through all sorts of trouble and pain, even to His death on the cross, for no other reason but to make us good. This will help us to understand why He is called the Son of God, the Saviour of men.

(3) And children should learn to know that there is in the heart of every one of us something which tells when we have done right or wrong, which makes the colour come into our cheeks when we have said what is not true, something which we must treat with honour and respect both in ourselves and others. What is this? There are many names by which you will hear it called in after life, but there is one name which we speak of almost in a whisper, because we do not like to think or speak of it as if it were a common thing. We call it 'the voice of God,' the invisible Power all around, which also is within us—the 'Breath' or the 'Spirit of God,' which we cannot see any more than we can see our

own breath or spirit—and because it is so good we call it 'the Holy Spirit of God.' And from this 'Breath or Spirit of God' comes all the good not only in ourselves but in other people; and children cannot learn too early to admire and love all that is admirable and lovable in the men, women, and children that they see around them. They may, perhaps, also be able to learn the great lesson that there are things to be admired and loved in people they do not like, in people that hurt and annoy them, or even in those whom they ought to avoid. And if, as sometimes happens, children are brought up in other countries where they see that people do not always go to the same church, or utter the same prayers as they and their parents, they may learn thus early a lesson which they never will forget—namely, that our heavenly Father has those who serve Him and do good in many different ways, but still in and by the same Good Spirit.

II. These are the chief things which we ought to learn from our catechism as to what the young should *believe*. And now, what must we teach them as to what they should *do*? St. John, when he was a very old man, so old that he could not walk, and could hardly speak, used to be carried in the arms of his friends into the midst of the assembly of Christians, and then he would lift himself up and say, 'Little children, love one another;' and again, 'Little children, love one another;' and again, 'Little children, love one another.' When asked, 'Have you nothing else to tell us?' he replied, 'I say this over and over again, because if you do this there is nothing more needed.' Now, that is something like what I would say to you. What you have to be told to do is very simple. It is that you should be kind and loving to one another, for then you will be loving towards God, because you will be doing that which He most desires. Try not to vex or tease your smaller brothers or sisters; try to help them when they are in difficulty; do not be jealous of them; do not tell stories against them; above all, do not lead them into mischief, because the worst harm you can do to a young child is to tempt him to do what is wrong. If he once begins you cannot stop him, and many years afterwards he will remember with bitter grief and indignation that you were the first to lead him astray into evil ways. A lie that is told, a deceit that is practised, a bad word that is heard, a bad act that is lightly spoken of, often enters into the mind of a young child, and remains there all his life. There is a proverb which says,

'Little pitchers have long ears;' and it means that little children often hear more than you think they hear, and keep in their memory things which you think they must have forgotten. It is the same, in other words, as a Latin proverb, which those boys who understand Latin will translate for themselves—*maxima debetur pueris reverentia*. The greatest reverence, the greatest fear should restrain us from doing anything by false, or vulgar, or foolish words to spoil the conscience, or the taste, or the character of a little boy. You know what you mean by a spoiled picture, or a spoiled book; the colours are blurred, the leaves are rumpled. That is what we mean by a child whose character is spoiled or stained by the foolish indulgence or neglect of those about him. Parents, try not to spoil your children. Children, try not to spoil one another; and take care not to be spoiled yourselves. That is one of the most important ways of fulfilling St. John's precept both for old and young, 'Little children, love—do not spoil—one another.' And there is another part of this precept which children should be taught: it is that love and kindness include not only our brothers and sisters and relatives, but also poor people who are in suffering or want; and not only these, but also the poor dumb creatures that depend upon us. Never be rude to any poor man or woman because they are in rags, or because they look and talk differently from ourselves. Never be cruel to any dog, or cat, or bird. There was once a very cruel Roman emperor—cruel to men, women, and children—who, when he was a little boy, used to amuse himself by tormenting flies. Perhaps if he had been stopped then he would not have had his heart hardened against his fellow-men.

III. And now how are you to be strengthened to believe and to do these things? There are many ways, but I will mention only two. By reading good books and by learning good prayers.

(1) Good books. First of all, the best parts of the Bible; for even in the best of all books, the Bible, there are some parts more useful, more easy, more likely to stand the trials of time than others. Learn these, teach these, and you will then find that the more difficult parts will not perplex those who in their early childhood have had a firm grasp of those parts of which the truth and beauty belong not to the vesture that is folded up and vanisheth away, but to the wisdom and grace which endure for ever. And of other good books, let the stories of the good and great men of our own or former times be fixed in our remembrance.

How many such stories there are, which, as Sir Philip Sydney said of Chevy Chase, stir our souls and spirits as with a trumpet! How many are there which will make our blood boil against the evil-doer, or our hearts beat with admiration for generous and noble deeds! There was a famous French soldier of bygone days whose name you will see written in this Abbey on the gravestone of Sir James Outram, because in many ways he was like Bayard. Bayard was a small boy, only thirteen, when he went into his first service, and his mother told him to remember three things: 'first, to fear and love God; secondly, to have gentle and courteous manners to those above him; and thirdly, to be generous and charitable, without pride or haughtiness, to those beneath him:' and these three things he never forgot, which helped to make him the soldier 'without fear and without reproach.' These are the stories which are part of the heritage of all the families of the earth, and ought to be cherished from the first to the last.

(2) And what must we teach, what must be learnt about prayer? Let no parent forget, let no child forget, to say a prayer, however short, at morning and at evening. It will help to make you better all the day. The Lord's Prayer will never fail

you. The child will be able to understand it, the old man will find it expressing all that he wants. And there is also that form of prayer which is expressed in hymns. There are hymns which can be remembered better than anything else, and which in restless, sleepless nights of pain and suffering will come back to our minds, many, many years after they were learnt in childhood. Amongst these let me recommend the Morning and Evening Hymns, written by one of the best of Englishmen, Bishop Ken—the first beginning, 'Awake, my soul, and with the sun;' and the other, 'Glory to Thee, my God, this night.' Not long ago I was visiting an aged and famous statesman,[1] and he repeated to me, word by word, the Evening Hymn, as he had learnt it, he told me, from his nurse ninety years before. So may it be with you, my dear children, not only with hymns, but with the other good things which you may learn now, and perhaps when you are like that old, very old man, grown gray in the service of his country, and full of years and honours, you may remember that when you were children you heard something which you have not forgotten on the festival of St. John, on the eve of Innocents' Day, in Westminster Abbey.

[1] Lord Stratford de Redcliffe.

IX.

TALITHA CUMI.

(December 28, 1880.)

Let me take this evening the story of our Saviour's kindness to a little girl. There was in Capernaum a well-known house where lived one of the chief officers of the synagogue. His name was Jairus. In that house was one only child, a little daughter of twelve years old, just at the age when a child has had time to endear itself to its parents, when its character first comes to be seen and known. The child was thought to be dying. The father heard that the Great Healer had just crossed the lake. He was feasting in the house of Levi, the publican. The father rushes in; he falls at His feet; —he entreats Him to come and save his daughter. The Lord arose; that little life was as precious in His sight as the souls of those whom He was convincing by His divine wisdom. He who said,

'Suffer the little children to come unto Me,' was as eager, if one may so say, to soothe the sick bed of this small Galilean maiden as though He had nothing else to do. For Him the thought of human sickness, the call of a suffering parent, was the most sacred of human duties. He came at once. All along the shore and all through the streets He had to force his way through the dense crowd, thronging ever more and more closely round Him. Whilst He thus struggled with the crowd, a messenger broke through the press with the sad tidings that it was too late. 'Thy daughter is dead.' Amidst the surging of the crowd, and above the hum of many voices, the Master's wakeful ear heard the whisper of the messenger. He bade the father still keep up his heart. 'Fear not,' He said, 'only believe.' 'Fear not,' He says to all anxious mourners. 'Fear not the dark and dreary void into which thy loved one has passed. Fear not that God will desert thee in thine hour of need. Fear not but that thou wilt once more see the child, the parent, the brother, the sister thou hast lost. Only believe in the lovingkindness of God our Saviour. Only believe that He who makes the flowers to spring and the buds to come forth again, will raise that little flower, will help that bursting blossom of the human soul.' He reaches the house. The hired mourners of Eastern countries are already there, wailing and shrieking, as is their wont. He put them all aside. He said to the parents, 'She is not dead, but sleepeth'; words that have often brought comfort to parents hanging over the face of their dead child in the hope of the general resurrection; words that are written in this church, on the pedestal of one of the children of the great family of Russell, who died in the reign of Queen Elizabeth. He touched the hand of the child, as she lay on her couch as if in the sleep of death. He addressed her in words which have been handed down literally. It is doubtful, in His discourses generally, what language our Saviour spoke—whether Greek or Syriac; but here, at any rate, the Syriac words are given. They are, 'Talitha cumi'; that is, 'My little lamb, my little pet lamb, rise up.' With these endearing appellations He roused the sleeping soul. By these He showed to the parents that He was one with them in their parental love, in their domestic joy as well as in their domestic sorrow. And she came again to life, and was to them as before.

Now let me apply this both to parents and children. Parents, remember what a gift, what an inestimable gift, is given to you in the soul of a little child; how its playful ways are to you the special gift of God. Think what a sight it is to see an innocent little girl; reflect how to any one except the most brutal of mankind such a sight banishes all thoughts of filthy language or foul deeds; remember that the tenderness and gentleness which the sight of such a little girl awakens is one of the best parts of your nature. If any of you doubt whether it is in you to be self-controlled and masters of yourselves, remember that, unless you are very bad indeed, you must be so in the presence of such a little being. Sir William Napier describes, in his 'History of the Peninsular War,' how affecting it was to see, at the battle of Busaco, in Portugal, a beautiful Portuguese orphan girl coming down the mountains, driving an ass loaded with all her property through the midst of the armies. She passed over the field of battle with a childish simplicity, scarcely understanding which were French and which were English, and no one on either side was so hard-hearted as to touch her. And let me give two stories which show how the strongest men are open to those tender kindly feelings which little children are given by our heavenly Father to promote in all of us. That same Sir William Napier once in his walks met with a little girl of five years old sobbing over a pitcher she had broken. She in her innocence asked him to mend it. He told her that he could not mend it, but that he would meet her trouble by giving her sixpence to buy a new one, if she would meet him there at the same hour the next evening, as he had no money in his purse that day. When he returned home he found that there was an invitation waiting for him, which he particularly wished to accept. But he could not then have met the little girl at the time stated, and he gave up the invitation, saying, 'I could not disappoint her, she trusted in me so implicitly.' That was the true Christian gentleman and soldier. Another example is that of Martin Luther, one of the fiercest and most courageous men that ever lived. But when he thought of his little children, especially of his little daughter, he was as gentle and kind as any woman. His daughter Magdalen died when she was thirteen years of age, and it is most affecting to read his grief, and, at the same time, his resignation. 'Magdalen, my little daughter, thou wouldst gladly stay with thy father here, and thou wouldst also gladly go to thy Father yonder.' 'Ah! thou dear little thing, thou shalt rise again, and shine like a star; yea, like the sun.' 'Her face, her words, cleave to our heart, remain fixed in its depths, living and dying—the words and looks of that most dutiful child. Blessed be the Lord Jesus Christ, who called, chose, and magnified her. I would for myself, and all of us, that we might attain to such a death; yea, rather, to such a life.'

And you, children, these words are also addressed to you. 'My little lamb,' the very word tells to you how precious you are to the Good Shepherd. Arise, get up, bestir yourself! get up from any slothful habit, from any idle, selfish habit you have formed. Let His voice reach your innermost heart, and raise you from the deepest sleep.

There was a boy who used to carry parcels from a bookseller to his customers. He went every day trudging through the streets with a heavy parcel of books under his arm, and one day he was sent to the house of a great duke with three folio volumes of Clarendon's 'History of England.' The parcel was so heavy, his shoulders were so tired, that as he passed through Broad Sanctuary, opposite Westminster Abbey, he laid down the load, and sobbed at the thought that there was nothing higher in life for him to look forward to than being a bookseller's porter. Suddenly he looked up at the great building which towered above him. He thought of the high thoughts and the great men enshrined within it. He brushed away his tears, replaced the load on his shoulder, and walked on with a light heart, determined to bide his time. And his time came at last. He became one of the best and most learned of our Indian missionaries.[1]

There was a little girl living with her old grandfather. She was a good child, but he was not a very good man, and one day when the little child came back from school he put in writing over her bed, '*God is nowhere*'; for he did not believe in the good God, and he was trying to make the little child believe the same. What did the little girl do? She had no eyes to see, no ears to hear, what her grandfather tried to teach her. She was very small; she could only read words of one syllable at the time; she rose above the bad meaning which he tried to put into her mind; she rose as we ought all to rise, above the temptation of our time; she rose into a higher and better world; she rose because her little mind could not do otherwise, and she read the words, not '*God is nowhere*,' but '*God is now here*.' That is what we all should strive to do. Out of words which have no sense, or which have a bad sense, our eyes, our

[1] Dr. Joshua Marshman.

minds, ought to be able to read a good sense. The old grandfather was touched and made serious, and we ought all of us to be made serious in like manner by the innocent questions and answers of our little children. *God is now here.* God is now, at this moment, watching over them and us. God is here, in this very Abbey, watching over the little children here assembled. God is in your homes, in your play, in your prayers, listening to you, as He is in this church, and He says to each one of you, to each one of us, 'Talitha cumi'—My little lamb, rise, mount up, be better this year than you were last year. Mount up, become better and wiser; mount up, rise up, as if you were climbing a long ladder; mount up, rise up, as if you were climbing a high mountain, and then you will be able to read those words, '*God is nowhere,*' in their truest sense. They mean that God is in no particular place. That is true; but it is not the whole truth—it is only half the truth, or, rather, it is, when taken by itself, the reverse of the truth. But when we make it '*God is now here,*' it becomes a great truth, for it tells us that because God is in no particular place, therefore He is in all places. God is now here, for God is always everywhere—your help in ages past, your hope for years to come.

X.

THE BEATITUDES.

(Saturday Afternoon, June 18, 1881.)

And seeing the multitudes, He went up into a mountain: and when He was set, His disciples came unto Him.

MATT. v. 1.

IT has been my wish, for some time since, to invite those who may be disengaged at this time of the year, and at this time of the day, to hear a few words which may perchance be useful to them on some of the serious matters connected with religion. The season of the Christian year which we are now entering upon is not marked by any solemnity which conspicuously attracts us: Christmas is over, Lent is over, Easter is over, Whitsuntide and Trinity Sunday are over, and there is nothing to break the long and even tenor which continues onwards towards Advent. The absence of any such particular solemnity appears to leave a vacant space in which we may possibly have an opportunity of calling attention to those truths through which alone all other facts and doctrines of the Christian religion are important.

I propose to speak of the Beatitudes pronounced by our Saviour on the characters in which He most delighted. They are all-important in several ways.

First, they open that discourse which, whatever may be the difficulties of particular parts of it, has always been recognised as the most important part of the New Testament. Nothing else in the Gospels, nothing in St. Paul's Epistles, can compare with the interest which attaches to the words derived from our Saviour's lips on this occasion. It is, as it has been well called, the Magna Charta of Christianity. These Beatitudes correspond in the Christian religion to the Ten Commandments delivered on Mount Sinai; they were intended by some good reformers of our Church Service to take the place of those Ten Commandments on the three great festivals of the Christian Church which are now past. They are not questioned, at least in their essential parts, by any of those various inquiries which have thrown some difficulty in the way of accepting this or that saying of our Saviour, this or that writing of His apostles.

Secondly, they put before us what are those qualities, and what are those results, which the Founder of our religion regarded as alone of supreme excellence. He does not say, 'Blessed are the Churchmen,' or 'Blessed are the Nonconformists'; He does not say, 'Blessed are the Presbyterians,' or 'Blessed are the Episcopalians'; He does not say, 'Blessed are the Methodists,' or 'Blessed are the Baptists'; He does not say, 'Blessed are the Roman Catholics,' or 'Blessed are the Protestants': but He says, 'Blessed are they who show those graces and virtues in their characters which may be found in every one of these communities, and under every one of these forms of belief.'

In proportion as we show any of these in our lives, we do what our Master tells us; in proportion as we do not show them, we fail in the purpose for which He lived and died for man. Often in revivals, and in confessions on death-beds, people ask, 'Are you happy?' 'Are you saved?' Christ gives us the answer: 'You are happy, you are saved, if you seek the happiness, first, of modesty; secondly, of compassion for sorrow; thirdly, of gentleness; fourthly, of an eager desire for justice; fifthly, of purity and singleness of purpose; sixthly, of kindness to man and beast;

seventhly, of pacific and conciliatory courses; eighthly, of perseverance in spite of difficulty.'

Again, the form of the 'Beatitudes,' as they are called—or, in other words, the declaration of the happiness of those who fulfil these things in their own lives—is perhaps the best way of leading us to practise those things. He does not say, 'Be merciful,' or 'Be pure in heart'; but He says, 'Happy are the merciful, happy are the pure in heart': that is to say, He points out that the happiness of which we all of us, rich and poor, are in search, can be found in one or other of these Divine qualities.

In this respect the same course was laid down by a great teacher of religion who existed among the heathen in the world of former times,[1] in words which it may perhaps be well for me to read to you, both because they are instructive in themselves, and also because they show the same deep feeling of desire that man should be happy and not miserable, which lay at the bottom of our Saviour's heart.

A disciple of that great teacher of whom I speak came to him and said, 'Many angels and men have held various things to be blessings when

[1] Buddha.

they were yearning for happiness: do thou declare to us the chief blessing.' This great teacher answered and said, 'Not to serve the foolish, but to serve the wise, to honour the worthy of honour—this is the greatest blessing. To dwell in the pleasant land, to have former good works to look back upon, and right desires in the heart—this is the greatest blessing. Much insight and instruction, self-control and pleasant speech, and whatever word be well spoken—this is the greatest blessing. To support father and mother, to cherish wife and child, to follow a peaceful calling—this is the greatest blessing. To bestow arms and live righteously; to give help to kindred, to do deeds which cannot be blamed—these are the greatest blessings. To abhor and cease from sin, to abstain from strong drink, not to be weary in well-doing—these are the greatest blessings. Reverence and lowliness, contentment and gratitude, the hearing of the law at due seasons—these are the greatest blessings. To be longsuffering and meek, to associate with those who are quiet, and have religious talk at due seasons—these are the greatest blessings. Self-restraint and purity, the knowledge of noble truths, the knowledge of the value of rest—this is the greatest blessing. On every side all are invincible who do acts like these; on every side they walk in safety, and theirs is the greatest blessing.'

I have read these words to you, not in order that they may take the place of our Saviour's teaching in the eight Beatitudes, far from it; but in order that you may see how, in this method of instruction, the great lights our God has sent into the world speak, on the whole, in the same voice. These are the Beatitudes of millions of our fellow-creatures in India. The Beatitudes of Jesus Christ are far simpler and nobler, but they both spring from the same spirit.

Fourthly, I have taken this subject of the states of mind which our Saviour calls 'blessed' because they furnish to us the great goal or end which will solve many difficulties in the great battle of life which we all have before us. This day is the anniversary of the battle of Waterloo—the greatest battle of modern times. It involved the question, Who should be master of the world? You know the object which sustained our soldiers in that great conflict. It was for the officers and generals the hope of vanquishing the great enemy of England; it was for all the soldiers the great object of fulfilling their duty to their country, and of obtaining that honour which is the soldier's great reward. These are noble motives, and they, no doubt, serve to nerve the heart and will against hardships and sufferings and death. We need not disparage such motives; but we are not all soldiers, and there are honours even greater than the reward of a grateful country. Those qualities of which our Saviour spoke are within the reach of all of us, and they amply serve to sustain us in all the conflicts of poverty and distress with which many of us are encompassed. There are, no doubt, many lesser kinds of happiness and virtue. There are, no doubt, many successes in life which attend on the swaggerers, the self-asserting, the commonplace, the listeners and retailers of gossip, the people who turn about with any evil wind that blows. But there is something beyond. In mountain countries there is, over and above all the lower hills, one range, one line of lofty summits which conveys a new sense of something quite different; and that is the range of eternal snow. High above all the rest we see the white peaks standing out in the blue sky, catching the first rays of the rising sun, the last rays of the sun as it departs. They are not the rounded hills which can be climbed by every one. They are not a range of extinct volcanoes, from which all fire has departed; they are the same always wherever we see them. Such are the Beatitudes. High above all earthly ordinary virtues, they tower into the heaven itself. They are white with the snows of eternity. And when the shades of sickness and sorrow gather round us, when other common characters become cold and dead, then those higher points stand out brighter and brighter; the glow of daylight can be seen reflected on their summits when it has vanished everywhere beside.

There are many examples of these different virtues. Sometimes in some rare cases we meet a man or a woman of whom it might always be said that you see all the eight Beatitudes written upon their faces. They belong to that circle of a very few by whom the whole world is made happier and better. But also we may meet with each of them separately; and we may, by dwelling on their separate existence, as exemplified by the living or the dead, be enabled to see that such virtues are possible; we may find comfort in dwelling upon them. I shall endeavour to take from those who are commemorated in this Abbey some one or two persons for each of these Beatitudes, who may give us something of a glimpse of what is meant by the 'pure in heart,' by the 'merciful,' by the 'poor in spirit,' by the 'peacemakers,' by those who 'hunger and thirst after righteousness,' and those who are 'persecuted for righteousness' sake.' If I can raise your minds to the appreciation of such virtues, if I can do this in any way so as to produce an impression upon you that we have something in life worth striving for, and that this Abbey, by its various examples, has something worth teaching, I shall not have spoken in vain.

XI.

THE BEATITUDES.

(Saturday Afternoon, June 25, 1881.)

Blessed are the poor in spirit: for theirs is the kingdom of heaven. Blessed are they that mourn: for they shall be comforted.—MATT. v. 3, 4.

I PROPOSE, in accordance with the plan which I laid down last Saturday, to take in order what are called the Beatitudes, in which our Saviour selected for His approbation the qualities which He most cherished. It will not be supposed that these qualities are equally found in all persons, or that their exemplification will always be equally applicable to Christians in different times of the world. The different Beatitudes, as it were, fill up the deficiencies which some of them leave; and they must be looked upon rather as describing to us points of character that are each in themselves good, and which when we see we cannot help admiring. It is the admiration of good qualities which is the best proof of spirit rising above matter. In whatever way these qualities are produced in man, whether inherited or acquired, it still remains certain that so long as there is a spark of enthusiasm enkindled for them in any human being, so long is the living proof retained of their undying excellence.

'Blessed are the poor in spirit.' This, like so many of our Saviour's words, is, as it were, a little parable in itself. As the poor man is with regard to the substance of this world, so is the 'poor in spirit' with regard to the various attractions of the soul and spirit. Blessed are the unselfish; happy are those who live for others, and not for themselves; happy are those among us who leave a large margin in their existence for the feelings which come to us from what is above, and also from what is around us. We know what a man is when inflated by the sense of his power, his wealth, and his intellect; how he goes about the world asserting himself, claiming everything on which he can lay his hands as his own. That is the man whom we may call purse-proud in spirit, rich with the prosperity and the aggressiveness of a powerful, wealthy man. The quality which our

Saviour admired was the reverse of this. It is to be found among the rich as well as among the poor, although, perhaps, poverty more conduces to it than riches. There was a story in old times told of a severe, cynical philosopher visiting the house of one who was as far his superior in genius as in modesty. He found the good philosopher living in a comfortable house, with easy chairs and pleasant pictures round him, and he came in with his feet stained with dust and mud, and said, as he walked upon the beautiful carpets, 'Thus I trample on the pride of Plato.' The good philosopher paid no attention at the time, but returned the visit, and when he saw the ragged furniture and the scanty covering of the floor of the house in which the other ostentatiously lived, he said, 'I see the pride of Diogenes through the holes in his carpet.' Many a one there is whose pride is thus shown by his affecting to be without it ; many a one whose poverty, whose modesty in spirit, can best be appreciated by seeing how the outward comforts and splendour of life can be used by him without paying any attention to them.

There is another way in which this unselfish feeling expresses itself—feeling for what is above us. 'Reverence,' Shakespeare says, 'is the angel of the world.' It is the angel of the world by smoothing and softening, and bringing into their right proportions, all the jarring elements of the human mind and human heart. It is what Burke described as produced by the entrance into this Abbey. 'The moment we enter into the Abbey,' he said, 'the very silence seems sacred'; and Wordsworth says:

> Be mine in hours of fear
> Or grovelling thought to seek a refuge here;
> * * * *
> Where bubbles burst, and folly's dancing foam
> Melts if it cross the threshold.

Some one has described how a great American orator and statesman, Webster, first entered the Abbey. He walked in, he looked around him, and he burst into tears. That is the acknowledgment of something undefined, mysterious, superior to ourselves, and superior to all common things, which is the root of all religion, and which springs from that modesty and humility of spirit which is described in the first Beatitude.

It is well said that 'theirs is the kingdom of heaven.' We do not, perhaps, perceive at once the success of those who are thinking of this or of higher things; but, nevertheless, in the long run it is sure to be theirs. There is a story told of a Welsh chieftain, who, on coming with his followers to a river, said, 'He who will be master must first make himself a bridge'; and he carried them, one after another, on his back until they reached the opposite shore. That is what we must all do. We must make ourselves the slaves of others, doing their work, securing their interests; if we wish to be in a high sense their lords and masters, we must be, all of us in our way, the servants of the public, not by doing their bidding, but by defending their interests; not by listening to their follies, but by seeking their good. There are two characters whose memory is enshrined in this church, who may be chosen out of many as instances of unselfish qualities. One is its first founder, Edward the Confessor. There was nothing in him of ability or power to commend him; he had just one single merit, that he thought more of the poor and the suffering than he did of himself; and for that reason the poor and the suffering for long years afterwards remembered him with gratitude; and when the Abbey was rebuilt by Henry III., it was in commemoration of these unselfish qualities of the last Saxon king. Another example is to be seen, of a very different kind, at the very extremity of the nave, where is a monument erected to a young philosopher, a clergyman, who, in the short space of a life which lasted only twenty-one years, made discoveries in science of a most surprising kind. His name was Jeremiah Horrocks. There was one thing which he felt, however, had a higher claim upon him even than science. It was the doing his duty in the humble sphere in which he found himself; and when he was on the eve of watching the transit of the planet Venus across the sun, and was waiting with the utmost keenness of observation for this phenomenon, he put all these thoughts aside, and went on the Sunday on which this sight was to be observed to perform his humble parish duty in the church where he was pastor. He mentions it in his journal in words which are now written over his monument: 'Called aside to greater things, which ought not to be neglected for the sake of subordinate pursuits.' Subordinate, secondary, in one sense, those pursuits could not be, for they were the discovery of the glory of God in the greatness of His works; but subordinate, in another sense, they were, for they came across, in that instance, the single-minded discharge of the duty which he owed to his parishioners and to his Divine Master. It was a true example of what an old poet has called 'high humility.'

Whatever you have to do, do it, whatever and however great may be things that would take you from it.

I turn to the next Beatitude, which falls in not unnaturally with this. It is 'Blessed are they that mourn.' The whole Abbey is indeed filled with the shadows of those that mourn. Every funeral, or almost every funeral, even the most splendid that takes place within these walls, has some sincere and heart-rending sorrow involved in the separation of death; always, or almost always, I have observed there have been sad faces in the long funeral processions which have accompanied the great and famous to their end; sad faces indifferent to the splendour of the scene around them, and lost in the thought of the dear friend or father or husband or son who had gone down into the dark grave. 'What,' we ask again and again—'what is the object of these dreadful sorrows? What is the gracious purpose which may be intended in these repeated strokes of human calamity?' It is hard to say; but thus much we may say—that if every one were to lift up his mind to the thoughts which arise at such moments, he would be in a condition far indeed raised above the frets and cares and sins of common life. There is in the grief of such times a tranquillising, solemnising, elevating wisdom, which transports even the most hardened amongst us into a region beyond himself. Any one who thinks how greatly he would regret bitter or foolish words or acts toward the dead as they lie before him, has a constant reminder that such acts and words are against the best spirit of a man as he actually lives and moves among his fellows. Think of what you are in sorrow. That is a true likeness of the high thoughts that we ought to have, that we may have always. In this sense, therefore, we may truly say that in the mourning of which this house of God is the constant memorial, there is a true source of comfort which never can be effaced. Because it is the temple of silence and reconciliation, it is the temple of God and the home of man. One touch of nature, it is said, makes the whole world kin; but it is because one touch of nature lifts us up into that higher and nobler state in which we are kindred of each other, because we then feel that we are kindred also with God. All the graves in the Abbey more or less convey this lesson. Let me name one, which has nothing else to commend it except its suggestive sorrow. It is in the Cloisters, where the parents have written on a tablet over their little girl, 'Jane Lister, dear child, died October 7, 1688.' That is all. It was at the time when every one was thinking of the stirring events which were leading to the revolution of 1688, but these parents thought of nothing else than their dear little child; their hearts were not on earth, but in heaven, where they hoped that she was. We cannot doubt that in so mourning they were comforted.

XII.

THE BEATITUDES.

(Saturday Afternoon, July 2, 1881.)

Blessed are the meek: for they shall inherit the earth. Blessed are they which do hunger and thirst after righteousness: for they shall be filled.—MATT. v. 5, 6.

I PROCEED with my statement of those whom our Saviour has called 'happy.' 'Blessed are the meek.' Those of you who have followed the changes made in the translation by the Revised Version, will have observed that these Beatitudes are left entirely unchanged; and this is due to the great solemnity which attaches to the words. But in this instance the word 'meek' hardly expresses the quality which is meant in the original. It is too passive a word; it does not sufficiently represent the active character which is intended. Those of you who can understand French will recognise this in the French translation: '*Bienheureux sont les débon-*

naires'; that is to say, 'Happy are the gracious, graceful, Christian characters who, by their courtesy, win all hearts around them, and smoothe all the rough places of the world.' Perhaps 'Blessed are the *gentle*' would best express it. If we give to the word 'gentle' all the meanings that it properly implies, it is the opposite of 'vulgar,' 'coarse,' 'barbarian'; it is the 'delicate,' 'refined,' 'civilised,' 'chivalrous.' We know its meaning when it is mixed up with another word, as in 'gentleman,' or 'gentleman-like.'

Our Saviour on one occasion said, 'Come unto Me; for I am meek and lowly in heart.' It really was, 'For I am *gentle*'; and it is said by an old poet of our Saviour that He was 'the first true gentleman that ever breathed.' Both the word 'gentle' and the word 'gentleman' rise very high above the common acceptation of the term. A peasant, an artisan, if he has this gracious quality of feeling for others, the courteous eagerness to avoid offence, may be as great a gentleman, in the true sense of the word, as any duke or any prince. 'He was a very perfect, gentle knight,' was the description given by Chaucer of a true gentleman in his day; and the words may be applied to one of our own time who is buried in our Abbey—George Grote, the historian of Greece, whose urbanity lives in the recollection of all who knew him.

These are the kind of qualities which penetrate into every corner, and which may be, therefore, truly said to inherit the whole earth. How very much may be done by a kind answer at a railway station by a railway porter! How very much pleasure, and even happiness, may be given by the policeman at the corner of the streets! How fully the duties of life are transformed into graces and pleasures by such gentle acts!

It has been sometimes said of persons, both in high stations and in humbler stations, that, next to being Christians, the great thing was that they should be gentlemen; that even if they were not called Christians, it was a great comfort to feel that one had a gentleman to deal with. And the happiness they distribute returns on themselves; for what can be more charming than to be gifted with those divine qualities which pass, one hardly knows how, into the rough feelings and habits of those around us, and diffuse all about us an atmosphere of gratitude and contentment—the determination not to give or take offence; the instinct that tells us that it is our business to pay attention especially to the neglected, and not to think only of the great? These are qualities which we may well call blessed, which may be found both in man and woman; and an example of it I will choose from this Abbey is a lady who lived more than 300 years ago. Her tomb may be seen in Henry VII.'s Chapel, and it is the most beautiful and venerable figure that this church contains. It is Margaret, the mother of King Henry VII., who is said, by her gracious and gentle manners, to have attracted all hearts towards her. 'Every one that knew her'—so it was said in her funeral sermon,—'every one that knew her loved her, and everything that she said or she did became her.' She was full of noble thoughts for her country; she counted it to be her sacred duty to end the Civil War of the Roses by securing the marriage of her son with Elizabeth of York. She founded colleges of learning at Cambridge; she bequeathed money for the poor of Westminster; and, as if to show how the gracious and beautiful conduct which was so characteristic of a lady in the highest walks of life could descend to the humblest station, she used to say that if the Christians would combine against their common enemy the Turk, she would undertake to go as their washerwoman. She felt, no doubt, that she could carry the dignity of a lady into that humble sphere: and, in like manner, every washerwoman or servant in this church might perform their duties of laundress and servant with the true grace and dignity of a lady.

The next quality which our Saviour blesses is thus expressed: They who 'hunger and thirst after righteousness.' He does not say, 'Those who have attained righteousness,' but those who have a hungering and craving after that which they perhaps have not reached, which they perhaps never, in this life, may fully attain to, but which to seek after is the truest ambition of the children of God.

When we look out into the world, when we see how much there is of falsehood and injustice and oppression all around, there is one consoling thing; and that is to see some who are filled with an earnest desire to make things better than they are.

There was a band of youthful scholars who met many years ago in Germany, and they bound each other by a simple resolution that they would not die until they had done something to leave the world better than they found it. There is such a thing, we know, as thirst after knowledge. Every one knows what a craving there exists, even amongst the humbler classes, for knowledge and learning. And the same figure of 'thirst' best expresses the ardent feeling of the soul for a nobler and purer life than that which we now have. 'Like as the hart'—like as the stag— 'desireth water brooks, so longeth my soul after Thee, O God.' We may have read how a stag—a stricken solitary deer, with the tears streaming down its cheeks, panting and heaving with its weary toil at the end of its day's long chase—plunges into the mountain torrent to bathe its worn-out limbs, or revels in the refreshing lake. It is a likeness of what, in common life we recognise—the thirst of the soldier on his march as he approaches the rushing river; the thirst of the politician, after his weary nights and days of toil, for moments of repose; the thirst of the labourer and the artisan after a long day's work. There is a representation in the Catacombs, on one of the Christian tombs, of a stag drinking eagerly at the silver stream, figuring the first sign of the Christian life.

This is the true likeness of hungering and thirsting after righteousness. When we are toiling towards the close of our earthly course, or in any especial period of it; when we feel stifled by the sultry and suffocating sense of the hardness and selfishness of the world about us; when our breath is, as it were, choked by the trifles and forms and fashions of the world we live in, or our ears deafened by the clattering of the world's vast machinery, we may still join the cry, 'I thirst for the refreshing sight of any pure, upright, generous spirit; I thirst for the day when I may drink freely of God's boundless charity; I thirst for the day when I shall hear the "sound of abundance of rain," and see a higher heaven than that which now incloses us round.'

Happy are they who, when they see generous deeds, and hear of generous characters higher than their own, long to be like them. It is our business to keep up the chase; not to cease our efforts to quench this thirst; never to be 'weary in welldoing,' and to believe that in this hunger and thirst is the spring of all true religion.

There was once in this country and in this church a wild young prince, who selfishly indulged in all the enjoyments and passions of youth. By his father's death-bed he was brought to a sense of better things, and from that moment his soul went on constantly aspiring to higher and severer courses of duty. It was King Henry V., whose tomb you may see behind Edward the Confessor's Chapel.

He especially attended to the complaints of the poor, and those who had none to help them. Unlike his ancestors and his kindred, he never swore any profane oath. He had only two words to express the strength of his determination and show what his resolution was. When anything was proposed to him that was wrong, his one word was 'Impossible'; when anything in the shape of a duty came before him, he had only one word, 'It must be done.' During many days his life as a soldier was unlike what one would desire; but he almost always had before him the sense of holier things; and when at last his end grew near, his dying words were, 'Build thou the walls of Jerusalem'; and, as if speaking to the evil spirit that had haunted his youth, he cried, 'Thou liest! thou liest! my heart is for the Lord Jesus Christ.' This, in times long ago, was an example how they which 'hunger and thirst after righteousness' can be filled—can be satisfied, at last, with the hope of having mastered their evil passions, and attained to that conquest over themselves which is more glorious than conquest over their enemies.

There are many others in this church who may recall to our minds the same thoughts as we wander round it—many who had before them a great and bright idea of human life, and who did something to realise it; such as those who laboured for the abolition of the slave trade, like Granville Sharp, Zachary Macaulay, and Wilberforce; those, also, who laboured for the revival of more serious thoughts and more just principles of action amongst their countrymen, like John and Charles Wesley. Let us seek to aspire in some degree towards their goodness, and humbly trust that, when we wake up from our long sleep, we may awake after their likeness and the likeness of the God whom they followed, and may be 'satisfied with it.'

XIII.

THE BEATITUDES.

(Saturday Afternoon, July 9, 1881.)

Blessed are the merciful: for they shall obtain mercy. Blessed are the pure in heart: for they shall see God.—
MATT. v. 7, 8.

'BLESSED are the merciful.' This especially illustrates what I said at the beginning of these discourses, that the object of each of the Beatitudes is to bring out the beauty of one particular quality without commending the other qualities which may exist in the same character with it. We see many men of very imperfect morality, and yet in whom this quality of mercy is such as to make us feel that, if it were universal amongst mankind, the whole world would be the happier for it, and that in those in whom it is found it is a redeeming virtue in the proper sense of the word—a virtue which redeems from condemnation and detestation the whole character in which it is found embedded. It is said that Lord Brougham made a resolution that he would count that day no day on which he had not done some one act of kindness towards some one fellow-creature. Lord Brougham was a man of many faults; but, if this resolution were sincerely made and sincerely acted upon, it is wonderful how much good it implies in the course of his long life. We see the same thing by examples where the reverse has been the case, where men have so hardened their hearts, or had their hearts so hard from the beginning, that they are steeled against all approaches to pity and compassion. Look at the cases of the betrayal of innocent girls to their ruin. Much else may be said of these cases; but one thing is that which the prophet urged against David—that he had no pity.

Look, again, at the case of assassinations—those assassinations which during the last few months have become so formidable. I do not now speak of the unsettling of all the bonds of society; I speak only of the total want of compassion and mercy which they show towards the individuals who are the victims of this frenzy. The Emperor of Russia [1] was a man with the same affections and

[1] Alexander II. assassinated March 13, 1881.

feelings as yourselves, with sons and daughters as you have; the President of the United States[2] had friends and family, who are dearly attached to him. It is said that the assassin did for a moment waver, because he felt a passing weakness in the presence of the wife whom he was about to deprive of a husband. We often say that Emperors, Kings, and Presidents are 'the same flesh and blood' as ourselves, meaning that they have the same infirmities and the same faults. In all these cases it is for the welfare and the safety of mankind that the common saying should have a more extended meaning given to it. Yes, it is because these great personages are the same flesh and blood as ourselves that they demand from us the kindly consideration which we should give to our own brothers, sisters, daughters, and husbands. Look, again, at the French Revolution and the Inquisition, and at the cruelties perpetrated in the name of Liberty in the one case and of Religion in the other. What was the cause of this? It was simply that the feeling of humanity, of mercy, had died out in the hearts of those unhappy men who rose to the highest places of authority, and that therefore they had no eyes to

---

[2] President Garfield, shot by an assassin, July 2, died September 19, 1881.

see and no ears to hear the tears and misery that they produced.

But let us take a wider sphere of compassion, which is due not only to human beings, but to all living creatures, whether of our own or of the animal creation. Martin of Galway! see what an immense circle of happiness he has diffused by reason of the Acts for restraining cruelty to animals which he carried through Parliament amidst obloquy of every kind, in defiance of the press, in defiance of popular opinion. How many a wearied horse, and jaded ox, and suffering dog, if they had voices to speak, would bless the name of Martin for the long-continued blessings which he has showered upon them! It is surely not too much to ask that this mercy or compassion to dumb animals should be made part of the very religion of childhood, that children may grow up to manhood with something of the same horror of cruelty to beasts and birds that they would feel with regard to each other.

There are two persons connected with this church whom I will specially name as examples of the virtue of mercy, even when surrounded by many qualities which we cannot admire or approve. One was the statesman, Charles James

Fox, whose monument you see in the nave of this Abbey. At his feet there kneels a negro, with clasped hands, and with the strongly marked physiognomy of his race, seeming to plead for the generous-minded benefactor, in whose heart, immersed as it was in public affairs and in private pleasures, the wrongs of those whom he had never seen awakened a spark of deep compassion and of just indignation, which causes him to be remembered in that noble band whom I mentioned last Saturday as hungering and thirsting after righteousness, but who was himself drawn towards that holy fellowship solely by this feeling of mercy and compassion. The other is Charles Dickens. There are many charges that might be brought against his style, and perhaps against his behaviour; but there was one quality which attracted to his grave the honour and the tears of English men and English women of all classes, especially the poor—it was that he had a tender heart for their sufferings, that he had that insight, which, perhaps, he was the first to display, into the squalor and temptations and wretchedness of their position, which won him an everlasting name among the benefactors of the humbler classes. Truly is it said that the merciful shall obtain mercy. We cannot believe that the generous and merciful acts of such men as these can ever be lost in the sight of God by reason of the other faults with which they are surrounded. It is the very quality on which our Saviour's blessing has been most distinctly pronounced. 'Forgive,' He says, 'and ye shall be forgiven.' 'Give, and it shall be given unto you.' And the feeling of posterity and the feeling of contemporaries is, after all, some slight index of what we may call in this respect the final judgment of God.

'Blessed are the pure in heart.' This is the next Beatitude, but one altogether different from that of which we have just been speaking. The one quality is found sometimes not coupled with the other; nevertheless, in this case also we feel that our Saviour's blessing has gone straight to the point. The words may bear a two-fold meaning—pure, disinterested love of truth, and pure and clean aversion to everything that defiles. Pure love of truth! How very rare, yet how very beneficent! We do not see its merits at once; we do not perceive, perhaps even in the next generation, how widely happiness is increased in the world by the discoveries of men of science who pursued them simply and solely because they were attracted towards them by a single-minded love of what was true. Look at Sir Isaac Newton, the most famous grave which this church contains. It was said by those who knew him that he had the whitest soul they had ever known—the whitest soul, perhaps, in other points also, but the whitest especially in this, that no consideration ever came across his desire of ascertaining and propounding the exact truth on whatever subject he was engaged. Corrupt elections, corrupt motives, are the very reverse of this Beatitude. Open your eyes! Take the mask off your faces!

Again, purity from all that defiles or stains the soul. Filthy thoughts, filthy actions, filthy words—we know what they are without attempting to describe them. How can the mind best be kept free from their intrusion? How is society best guarded from their corrupting influence? Let us take three examples from those who are buried or who have monuments in this church. Milton has not only told us that he was from his earliest youth entirely free from such defilements, but he imprinted it in such a manner in the words of his poems that no one can read those poems and admire them without feeling as if he had passed into a keen and frosty atmosphere, where all low and debasing thoughts vanish away. Look at his description of chastity in 'Comus'; look at his description of the purity of married life in 'Paradise Lost.' Are they not as a sword and shield with which we may defend ourselves against all the fiery darts of temptation? Addison, again, lived at a time when the profligacy which broke over England in the reaction against the too great severity of the Puritans overran and undermined all literature and all morality. Addison furnished a literature in which there was at once everything to please, and nothing to give countenance to those gross and dark images which had haunted the imagination of his contemporaries. It shows what can be done by one man in this respect, that Macaulay, who lies beside his statue, and who has written an essay to commemorate the benefactions which Addison bestowed upon England, has given foremost place to this, that Addison effected a great social reform, and reconciled wit and virtue after a long and disastrous separation, in which wit had been led astray by profligacy, and virtue by fanaticism. Wordsworth has the glory of having not only abstained from anything which can injure or defile the soul, but of fixing the mind upon those simple affections and upon those great natural objects of beauty and grandeur which are the best preservatives against any such attempts to corrupt and stain our existence. We sometimes hear it said that these dark and fleshly ideas are necessary accompaniments of genius or of poetry. Not so. In the case of Shakespeare, and even more remarkably in the case of Byron, what they have written that is low and filthy is not poetry, is not that which commends them for ever to the gratitude of their contemporaries and countrymen. It is in proportion as they are pure, in proportion as they are clean, in proportion as they are elevated above anything like such corrupt thoughts, that they become our guides and our delight.

And what is the reason that our Saviour gives for this blessedness of the 'pure in heart'? It is that 'they shall see God.' What is the meaning of this? It is that of all the obstacles which may intervene between us and an insight into the nature of the invisible and the Divine, nothing presents so coarse and so thick a veil as on the one hand a false, artificial, crooked way of looking at truth, and on the other hand the indulgence of brutal and impure passions; and nothing can so clear up our better thoughts, nothing leaves our minds so open to receive the impression of what is good and noble, as the single eye and the pure conscience; which we may not, perhaps, be able to reach of ourselves, but which are an indispensable condition of having the doors of our minds open, and the channel of communication kept free between us and the supreme and eternal fountain of all purity and of all goodness.

[This was Dean Stanley's last Sermon. It was preached on July 9, 1881, and he died on the 18th of the same month.]

XIV.

THE FAITHFUL SERVANT.

(Preached at Alderley, on February 10, 1856, on the death of Sarah Burgess, for thirty-eight years the devoted and beloved servant of the family of the Rev. Edward Stanley.)

Well done, good and faithful servant; thou hast been faithful over a few things: I will make thee ruler over many things: enter thou into the joy of thy Lord.—MATT. xxv. 23.

THE Parable from which these words are taken is one of the most important in the whole Bible. It describes mankind not only according to the general division of the good and bad; but according to those many varieties and divisions of character, pursuits, opportunities, which we actually see with our eyes in this world. 'The kingdom of Heaven is as a man travelling into a far country, who called his own servants and delivered unto them his goods; and unto one he gave five talents, to another two, and to another one, *to every man according to his several ability.*[1] Look round any congregation, any circle of our acquaintance, any family, this is exactly what we see; no two persons have the same gifts, or the same advantages; one has five talents, another has two, another has one. Scripture and experience speak here the same language; every one will feel that thus far he is sure from his own knowledge that what the Parable says is true. And to every one it has its lesson to give as it proceeds. Many passages of Scripture are intended to alarm the very wicked, or to console the very good; but this Parable is intended for by far the larger class, who are neither very good nor very wicked; whose sin consists not in doing what is wrong, but in neglecting to do all the good they might do with the gifts entrusted to them. Our Master is gone away into a far country. He has left His goods with us, to use or to neglect. He will not help us unless we help ourselves. It is no excuse to say that our opportunities were small, that we had but one talent, and that therefore we 'hid it in the earth': this was the very reason why we should have made the most of it, why we should have

[1] Matt. xxv. 14, 15.

'put it out to the exchangers,' so that when our Lord comes again 'He may receive his own with usury.'[2] As the Parable thus contains a warning to the unfaithful servants, so it contains an encouragement to all those faithful servants, be they high or low, who have traded with their talents, few or many, great or small. It reminds us that talents, used well and faithfully, bring with them, both in this world and in the next, their own great reward; that in the great toil and struggle of life the race is not to the swift nor the battle to the strong, but to those who out of little have made much, who out of weakness have perfected strength; who having been faithful over 'few things' have been made and will be made 'rulers over many things.'

This great truth, like all the truths and doctrines of Scripture, is best understood by example; by the knowledge of our own hearts, or by the knowledge of one with whose character and end we have been ourselves acquainted. Such an one we have known in her whose remains we last week committed to the grave; whose name, whose life, whose voice and countenance have been long familiar to almost all in this place; who was a

[2] Matt. xxv. 27, 28.

constant testimony to the truth of these words of our Saviour.

Let us consider what we may all of us learn from a character and a life which was not granted to us for nothing. It was itself one of God's gifts for our use. Let us see how we can still keep it amongst us, how we can still 'put it out to the exchangers': let us not 'hide it' in the grave which was 'digged in the earth'[3] to receive that which was 'of the earth, earthy,' but let us treasure up the memory of that part which was 'heavenly,' that, though we 'have borne the image of the earthy' to her last home, we may 'bear' with us 'the image of the heavenly,' till we also meet 'the Lord from Heaven.'[4]

What, then, was the talent which was committed to her keeping? Ah! who ever knew her will feel that in her was lost a true servant, a true friend, a true sister, a true mother; to many here, as to many elsewhere, she was the best likeness of Heaven, and heavenly things, that they had ever known. What was it that she thus faithfully used? and how did she use it?

Was it wealth, or station, or fame? No. She was born and bred in the humble rank of so many

[3] Matt. xxv. 18.   [4] 1 Cor. xv. 47, 48, 49.

amongst us. No books tell of what she did; no great means of guiding, or ruling, or helping others were granted to her: she died, as she had lived, 'not ministered unto, but ministering.' Or was it strength and health, such as enables many of us to bear much, and do much, 'rising up early and late taking rest, eating the bread of carefulness,' 'going forth to work and to labour till the evening'? No. You know well that these were not granted her; you remember well her fragile form, her wasted features, faint and weary with the journey of life before her years were half numbered; like a withered leaf, that a breath of wind might blow away in a moment. This was what she was outwardly. 'The flesh indeed was weak' and frail; but the 'spirit was willing'[5] and ready. It was this readiness and quickness of spirit which God had given to her, which, carefully trained by others, carefully trained by herself, carefully trained by God's grace, rose above all weakness and infirmity of body; rose above all humbleness and lowliness of station; rose above all selfishness of the flesh and of the spirit; and has risen, we may humbly trust, above the power of death and the grave.

[5] Matt. xxvi. 41.

Let us see, piece by piece, through her life, how this was carried out. Let me especially commend her example to the young amongst us. Such as they are now, such she was once. Let them think, as they hear me describe what she was, how they may at last be as we trust she is now. And first, in her earliest years, in the school of this parish, she laid the beginning of that ready quickness of which I have spoken. What she learned she learned well: what she did she did with her whole soul. There are those who can remember her as she sat working at her humble task, with that fixed attention which alone makes work good and sure. Here she first took in that interest in things around her, in things above her, which she never afterwards lost: here she first learned to know and value those whom afterwards it was the happiness of her life to serve, living or dying: here she first laid in that store of knowledge of hymns and sacred texts and chapters, which she never forgot in after times. Long, long afterwards, far away from this place, in years and months of illness, in the long nights when she would lie awake from pain and restlessness during her last sickness, she would find rest and comfort in repeating to herself the hymns and passages [6] from Scripture which she had learned in Alderley School. Consider this, my younger hearers, you who think it time lost to lay up in your memory what you will never again have the opportunity of gaining, remember that, here or at your homes, you have, now or never, the chance of receiving what will come back to you with usury in after years; that your solitary hours, your bed of sickness, will be cheered or darkened according as you have made the most of the one talent, small though it be, which God gives you in the school of your childhood.

From school she passed, as so many of you will pass or have passed, into service. For a short time she was in the service of your present venerable Minister. Then she passed into the family which for the remaining thirty-eight years of her life she never left. All that she was in that family it is not possible, it is not necessary for me fully to speak. How she was one with them in their joys and their sorrows, how every change of place and station

[6] It may be mentioned that amongst the passages thus learned, in which she took special delight, were the Sermon on the Mount, in the 5th, 6th, and 7th chapters of St. Matthew's Gospel; the 12th, 13th, and 14th chapters of the Epistle to the Romans; and the 3rd and th chapters of the Epistle to St. James.

was shared by her with them, you know almost as well as I do. You know how, through her, every intelligence which could affect us was felt by yourselves; how in her happiness or joy was reflected every good or evil fortune which befell every member of the family, far or near, old or young. But you can hardly tell how great is the blessing which such a union between master and servant sheds around on all who come within its influence. To know that in the midst of that household there sat one who, through all the changes and chances of life, thought far more of the interests and comfort and welfare of those whom she served than of her own; who never thought of what she wished or liked, but only of what they wished or liked; who in all sickness and distress, in all difficulty and prosperity, in all time of our tribulation, and in all time of our wealth, was ever ready with a bright smile, with a kind look, with a wise word, with a gentle touch, with a quick eye, to calm, to cheer, to assuage, to counsel; this was indeed a light shining in the darkness of this evil world. It was an example to those who served with her to see in her what they ought to be—not the servants only, but, 'as in the sight of the Lord,' the guardians, the friends, the support and stay of the interests of those whose interests could not be divided from their own. It was a never-failing source of refreshment and consolation to those whom she served, that whatever else changed in the world around, or within their circle, she was there, unchanging and unchangeable. When the heavens were dark around, and when troubles came thick and fast, or when the 'faithful seemed to fail from among the children of men,' one true heart was there, to prove that there is a constancy and a peace which the world has not given, and which the world cannot take away. It was a living parable to all, to remind us that what she was to her earthly master we all ought to be and may be to our heavenly Master. 'Behold, even as the eyes of servants look unto the hand of their masters, and as the eyes of a maiden unto the hand of her mistress.' This first part of the verse was the exact likeness of her constant life; would that we could all learn the conclusion that the Psalmist draws from it—' Even so our eyes wait upon the Lord our God until He have mercy upon us.'[7] In her the two services were united. Through her earthly service she wrought out her heavenly service also: but how forcibly does such an example bring before us what

[7] Psalm cxxiii. 2.

our relation should be to our heavenly Father, of whom 'every family in heaven and earth is named,'[8] making His will our will, His love our love, His joy our joy. Bear this in mind, all masters of households, who have known this or any like example of fidelity to your interests, 'knowing that ye also have a Master in Heaven.'[9] Bear this in mind all ye that are or will be servants, '*in singleness of heart* as unto Christ'; 'not with eye-service as men-pleasers, but as servants of Christ doing the will of God *from the heart: with good will* doing service *as to the Lord* and not to men; knowing that whatever good thing any man doeth, the same shall he receive of the Lord.'[1] Do not despise it, do not think it beneath you. The service of men, as the apostle thus tells you, may indeed be in the fullest sense the service of Christ: from your example lessons may be taught which would never be taught by anything else; from your faithfulness in a few things, those who in this world are rulers over many things may often learn lessons of humility, of faith, of love, which in their own stations they might else never have learned at all.

But there was yet another field in which 'our

[8] Eph. iii. 15. [9] Col. iv. 1.
[1] Eph. vi. 5, 6, 7, 8.

dear sister here departed' used to the uttermost all the talents that were committed to her. '*Our dear sister here departed.*' How touchingly, how powerfully, must those words have come to the hearts of those mourners, who stood round the grave last week ! 'Sister,' indeed, in no common sense, sister by all the ties of earthly relationship, sister by all the ties of Christian brotherhood, in all sisterly and family affections ; never ceasing to remember the place of her nativity, the home of her childhood, the friends of her youth, the father and mother who trained her in the way that she should go, the brothers and sisters whom she had faithfully loved, the brothers' children and the sisters' children, to whom she became, as it were, a second mother, as they grew up round about her. Others, often, become faithful servants in distant households ; and by degrees their early haunts know them no more ; lapse of years and change of place, without any fault of theirs, loosens, and dissolves the bond of ancient natural affection. Not so, my brethren, not so with her, whom you, as well as we, have now lost. Dear as were to her the interests of the family which she served, no less dear were the interests of the family from which she was born. She did not, as many do, make one duty the excuse for neglecting another duty; she fulfilled them both. The school, the church, the cottages of her native parish were always present with her; she never lost her old simple habits: she always delighted to return amongst you: she wrote to her absent family, often twice or thrice a week, what they wished or what they needed to hear: she always loved to talk of her early days, of her home beside the wood, of her prizes at school, of her kinsfolk and acquaintance. Long and tenderly she ministered to her aged mother: only a few days before her end, she spoke to me at length of her father's goodness and simple piety, of his daily prayers before he went to his work, of his reading of the Bible by his fireside, of a rebuke which he had given to her for a hasty expression in her childhood, by which she had never ceased to profit. When she came down amongst you, you know how she would gather the rising generation of her family around her: how she would give to her little nephews and nieces, as they stood beside her, words of wise counsel for this world and for the next; how she watched over their welfare; how she guarded and guided them onwards and forwards and upwards. You also know how deeply she had set her heart on laying her last remains amongst her own people, in the grave of her father and her mother. Long ago she had made those near her promise that whenever and wherever her last hour found her, she should be laid nowhere but here. And when at last it did approach with certainty, then her longing for her native place grew stronger; the recollection of the churchyard seemed to draw her homewards; and home at last she has been brought; her mortal remains to her home here on earth, her spirit to that home where the weary are at rest for ever.

It is not without cause that I speak of that strong family affection. It reminds you that she was truly your own, that whatever good she had was hewn out of the same rock, cast in the same mould as yourselves; what she was you may be; what she longed that you, her younger kinsfolk, might be, that, remembering her wishes, you ought to become, and, with God's grace, you may become hereafter. It reminds you also of the value of these affections: honour them, cherish them; they are not enough in themselves to guide us to Heaven, but they are the beginning of all heavenly and holy thoughts. The very desire which she expressed so strongly to be laid amongst you, is that same ancient feeling of which you read in the patriarchs and saints of old, who, when dying in strange lands, charged that their bones should be taken and buried with their fathers in the cave of Machpelah, in the land of promise : [2] so that even in death their union should not be broken. So may it long be with you : so may this place, this church, this churchyard, always draw you to each other, to those who have gone before us, and to God in Jesus Christ. . . .

It was only a short time before her end, that I asked her one day what was her favourite text in the Bible. Without a moment's hesitation she answered, and dwelt on every word as she repeated it : 'Come unto me, all ye that labour and are heavy laden, and I will give you rest. Take My yoke upon you, and learn of Me ; for I am meek and lowly in heart ; and ye shall find rest unto your souls. For My yoke is easy and My burden is light.' We have long known the text ; we read it often ; we hear it often ; whenever the sacrament of the Lord's Supper is administered we hear it : it needs no human recollections to add anything to the sweet music of its sounds, or to the abiding strength of its consolations. Yet even divine words like these may be brought nearer home to every one of us, if we have seen their comfort and their

[2] Gen. xlix. 29, 30 ; l. 25.

truth exemplified in any one whom we ourselves have known.

Ponder well the words ; and how naturally do they recall the image of her whose stay and support they had become. 'All ye that labour and are heavy laden.' How exactly does this describe her outward form and manner of life ! Think of her failing strength, her frequent pains, her slow step, vainly striving to keep pace with her active spirit ; think, especially as years advanced, of the toil and difficulty with which she dragged along her weary limbs, heavy laden with ever-increasing infirmity ; think of the brave struggle with which, under all this burden, she yet laboured and travailed to the last. Yet this life, so full as it might have seemed of pain and misery, was a life of true and constant happiness. Think of her once more : and you will see that she had indeed come to Him who said 'I will give you rest,' 'I will refresh you.' Think of that patient, contented, ever-brightening smile ; think of those kind, cheering, happy words, always ready for those who came in and went out amongst us ; recall her as she passed to and fro amongst her kindred here, always bent on doing some little act of thoughtful goodness, never forgetting, never omitting any : recall her as she sat silent and composed in her chair, plying her daily task or turning over the leaves of her little hymn-book or prayer-book ; remember the calm resignation with which, without fear, without excitement, she was ever expecting her latter end ; ever thankful for the mercies she had enjoyed through life, ever filled with the thought that the daily words of parting for her evening rest might be for the last time ; and you will indeed see that hers was the happiness and peace of one who had found 'rest to her soul' where only it can be found.

And how she had sought and found it? Still the words of her text guide us. She had 'taken His yoke upon her,' she had learned of Him who was 'meek and lowly of heart.' Humbly, faithfully, lovingly,—in childhood, in youth, in age,—in all the intercourse of life, she had striven to take upon her the yoke of His words, of His commandments, of His will. Steadily, firmly, she strove to be guided in all things, not by her own pleasure, not by her convenience, not by her feelings, but by a fixed sense of duty, of truth, of justice, of honest and loving obedience ; as ever in the presence of Him who is 'without variableness or shadow of turning,' in the service of Him who, as she delighted to remember, was 'Jesus Christ, the same yesterday, and to day, and for ever.'³ And this she did, labouring to be like Him in all 'meekness and lowliness of heart.' Loved, honoured, esteemed as she was by all around her, she never rose above her station ; she never joined together things that were incongruous or unsuitable ; she never grasped at power, or wealth, or consideration for herself; she bore always the same simple, humble heart, that she brought with her from her early childhood. By her lowliness only she was exalted ; by her meekness only she 'inherited the earth.'⁴

And of her most truly it may be said, that 'His yoke was easy, and His burden was light.' You who are young, you who are in full enjoyment of health and life, and spirits, you who think that a serious and religious life must be mournful and difficult, that the Lord whom you are called upon to serve is an 'austere and hard Master, reaping where he has not sown, and gathering where he has not strawed' ;⁵ look at what you know, remember what you have heard, of her who is gone from us. There was indeed much to make her life sad ; much, as I have said, of pain and suffering ; much of sorrow and mourning for the loss of those she

³ Heb. xii. 8.   This was also a favourite text of hers.
⁴ Matt. v. 5.   ⁵ Matt. xxv. 24 ; Luke xix. 21.

dearly loved ; for the parting from scenes and places where she had struck deep root ; much of anxious care that her duty might be fully performed. But every one who knew her will say, as she herself often said, that her life had been full of happiness. No innocent enjoyment passed within her reach, but that it lighted up her face with a cheerful gleam ; no means of adding to the comfort and pleasure of others was ever neglected by her ; to smooth down family trouble, to promote everywhere agreement and good-will, and brotherly and sisterly affection, was her constant aim. And the pleasure she gave to others was reflected back on herself. They, who live for others and not for themselves, are always rewarded by this very thing ; even if they have no joy themselves, they rejoice in the joy of others ; the health of others, the prosperity of others, the peace of others, becomes to them as it were in the place of their own health, covers their own adversity, enlightens their own obscurity ; like the apostle, of whom we have read in this day's service ;[6] 'as unknown, and yet well known ; as sorrowful, yet alway rejoicing ; as poor, yet making many rich ; as having nothing, yet possessing all things.' But more than this, there

[6] 2 Cor. vi. 9, 10.

was the joy within; 'the peace' of those 'whose mind is stayed on God.' It is the special blessing of the yoke of Christ, not only that it is easy, but that it makes all other things easy; it is the special blessing of the burden of Christ that it is not only light itself, but that it makes all other things light. So it was with her. Because she had taken upon her the yoke of Christ, therefore the yoke of service, which some find heavy and grating and painful, was to her easy and delightful; because she had taken upon her the burden of Christ, therefore the burden of care and the burden of sickness and suffering, became but as 'a light affliction, which was but for a moment, working for her a far more exceeding and eternal weight of glory.'[7] All around partook of the heaven which was within: there was no struggle against itself, for self was swallowed up in faith and love.

In the 35th[8] chapter of the Book of Genesis you may read a touching scene in the story of the Patriarch Jacob, which bears witness how from the earliest times all respect has been paid to such long and honourable service as that of which we are speaking. He had been a far wanderer in a strange country: he had seen many changes of good and

---

[7] 2 Cor. iv. 17. [8] Verses 6, 7, 8.

evil fortune, many forms of human character; he had come back to his native land; with his staff he had crossed over the Jordan many years before, and now he had become two mighty bands: and he came to Bethel in the land of Canaan, 'the place where God appeared to him when he fled from the face of his brother.' There he halted, in the middle stage of his journey; in the middle stage of the years of his pilgrimage through life; and there, we are told, 'Deborah, Rebekah's nurse,' the nurse that had come with his mother from her own people years before, 'she died and she was buried beneath Bethel, under an oak, and the name of it was called Allon Bachuth, that is, the oak of weeping.' Many griefs had befallen him in times past—many griefs were yet to befall him in times to come. But this grief was not to be forgotten. Under the old gray stones which had been set up in Bethel, the 'house of God,' where he first awoke to a consciousness of the presence of his Lord and Maker; under the shade of the aged oak-tree which from generation to generation had spread and would still spread its branches over the consecrated spot, the faithful servant of his father's house was laid; and the memory of the spot was long preserved, and under the oak of Deborah, beside the house of God, in many a distant time, the wayfarer would often rest, and remember the name of her whose remains reposed beneath.[9] Even so, my brethren, long may that spot be known and remembered where the faithful friend and servant of many years has been laid beside the well-known tree, under the ancient tower, in that quiet and secluded corner, which she knew and loved so well, in the grave of her parents and her kindred.

But let us think not only of the earthly grave and its earthly sorrows; let us think of all which that grave is intended to teach us; what thoughts not only of sorrow, but of joy and comfort and heavenly hope we may carry away with us, whenever we pass by it, or whenever we think of her who there sleeps her last sleep. It was indeed when we stood beside it last week, what Jacob called the grave of Deborah—'the oak of weeping' —'the oak of tears.' But it may also be to those who view it rightly, 'the oak of gladness,' 'the gate of Heaven';—the entrance into that joy which shall never pass away.

It costs us all a pang when standing at the open grave which is to receive the last remains of any

[9] 1 Sam. x. 3; 1 Kings xiii. 14.

near and dear to us, to 'give *our hearty thanks* to God for their deliverance from the miseries of this sinful world.' Yet when we consider in any case— when we consider in her case—what those miseries are from which she is now for ever set free, we shall be able to feel that the loss we so deplore is yet a cause of thanksgiving. Think what she has been spared ; think of her ' deliverance from the *burden*,' as it was fast becoming, the burden of the weak and suffering flesh : think of the successive pangs which would have entered like iron into that loving and devoted soul, had she lived, as in the ordinary course of human things she might have lived, to see one by one the departure of those whom she so loved and served on earth. Think also of the deliverance, for which she, if she could but speak, would give the deepest thanksgiving of all ; the deliverance from all those little infirmities, trials, temptations, with which even the best and most saint-like of us are compassed about in this mortal life. It is the peculiar trial of characters like hers, that they cannot bear to see anything done by others which they can by any possibility do themselves. In some this may arise from other causes —from love of power, from jealousy, from mistrust. In her this infirmity, so to call it, was occasioned not by reasons of this kind, but by the exactness, the nicety, the eagerness, of her desire to see all done in the best way in which she thought it could be done; from her great unwillingness, also, ever to take from others that service and that trouble, which she thought it to be her station and duty always to be rendering, never to be receiving. She knew well that she had this trial; and she spoke with humble hope that He who is perfectly just, and who knew whereof she was made, would judge and receive her, according to that 'faithfulness and truth,' in which she put her entire trust. But from this and all like trials, from this craving, never satisfied, after perfection on earth, we may feel sure that she is especially delivered in that world to which she has gone. There they 'who hunger and thirst after righteousness' are blessed, for there their longings shall at last be filled. There she will no more vex her righteous soul with the sight of good which she cannot accomplish, and of evil which she cannot prevent. There she will no more be fretted by the thought of ministrations imperfectly rendered, by the sight of good designs half finished. In that better world there is no pavement strewed with good intentions unfulfilled; in that world there will be no let or hindrance to the full service always given with all the energy of that love, which, as the apostle tells us, 'never fails'[1]—'for the throne of God and of the Lamb shall be in it; and His *servants shall serve Him.*'[2] Yes, my brethren, dim and distant, and 'seen through a glass darkly,' are all our notions of another world. Yet, if anything be certain respecting it, this is certain, that according to our faithfulness in a few things here, will be our rule over many things there. Her last words, uttered as if with a consciousness that her end was at hand, as she retired to rest on her last night, were, '*My work is done.*' Done it was, 'well done' on earth; but not done, rather still to be continued, and begun afresh, in the eternal state beyond.

In this world, our faculties, our gifts, our talents, are limited by outward circumstance, by humble station, by small fields of duty. Many who have acquired a great name in history have gained it not because they were better or wiser than others, but only because they had here greater and wider opportunities. Not so in the world to come. There the spirits of all will find their appointed services. Our heavenly home has room and verge enough for all the energy which in this narrow spot of earth

[1] 1 Cor. xiii. 8. [2] Rev. xxii. 3.

has been cramped and shackled down. In our Father's house are many mansions;[3] and in one or more of those many mansions the ever-increasing 'number of His elect' will, in ways which eye hath not seen nor ear heard, fulfil their Father's will. Then will be seen that union of rest and labour, of repose and active energy, in this world vainly though earnestly sought by all the true disciples of Him to whom rest and work are one. Both will then be possible; of both, we have the promise in those strains, few and far between, which reach us from that higher state. On the one hand, we 'hear a voice from heaven saying, Blessed are the dead which die in the Lord; for they *rest from their labours* :'[4] on the other hand, we see a vision as of living creatures 'round about the throne, which *rest not* day and night; and give glory and honour and thanks to Him that sits on the throne, who liveth for ever and ever.'[5] And again we hear the sweet plaintive tones of a still small voice, which saith, 'Come unto Me, all ye that labour and are heavy laden, and I will give you rest';[6] but it is mingled with the stirring, cheering, strengthening sounds, 'as it were of a trumpet talking with us':[7]

[3] John xiv. 2. [4] Rev. xiv. 13. [5] Rev. iv. 8.
[6] Matt. xi. 28. [7] Rev. iv. 1.

'Well done, good and faithful servant: thou hast been faithful over a few things, I will make thee ruler over many things. Enter thou into the joy of thy Lord.'

^b Matt. xxv.

www.ingramcontent.com/pod-product-compliance
Lightning Source LLC
Chambersburg PA
CBHW030258170426
43202CB00009B/795